Flashpoints

Editor: Harry Browne

France:
The May Events 1968

France:
The May Events
1968

Roger Absalom

Longman

76 0566139

Longman Group Limited
London

Associated companies, branches and representatives throughout the world

© Longman Group Ltd 1971
*All rights reserved. No part of
this publication may be reproduced,
stored in a retrieval system, or
transmitted in any form or by any
means, electronic, mechanical,
photocopying, recording, or otherwise,
without the prior permission of the
Copyright owner.*

First published 1971

ISBN 0 582 32810 1

Photoset and printed in Malta
by St Paul's Press Ltd

Contents

Sequel

Acknowledgements

We are grateful to the following for permission to reproduce copyright material:

B.P.C. Publishing Ltd., for extract from *Students and Workers* by John Gretton; the proprietors of *The Economist* for extracts from 'Strikes in France' 25.5.68., 'Genelle Agreements' 1.6.68., 'Gaullism after 10 years' by Norman Macrae 18.5.68. and 'The Cost of May' 16.8.69. from *The Economist*; the proprietors of *L'Express* for extracts by J.J. Servan-Schreiber 13.5.68., 'La bataille des 10,000 heures' 15.4.68., and 'La revolte des paysans' by Georges Suffert 9.10.68 from *L'Express*; the proprietors of *The Guardian* for an extract from 'Fight to break the gag on broadcast news' by Hella Pick 30.5.68. and an extract from 'Student Unrest in France' by Nesta Roberts 22.2.68. from *The Guardian*; author for extract from 'Going Far and far to go' by Peter Lennon from *The Guardian* 29.5.68; the proprietors of *Le Monde* for extracts by Alain Touraine 11.5.68., 'Quand les enrages vont au peuple' 'La pegre de Nantes' 29.5.68. 'Quand la France s'ennuie' by Pierre Viansson-Ponte 15.3.68 and an article by B. Girod de L'Ain 8.5.68. from *Le Monde*; the proprietors of the *New Statesman* for extracts from 'The Night of the Long Batons' by P. Johnson 17.5.68., 'The New Spectre Haunting Europe' by P. Johnson 24.5.68. 'Last Days of De Gaulle' by K.S. Karol 31.5.68., 'That Week in Paris' by Mervyn Jones 7.6.68. from the *New Statesman*; The *New York Review of Books* for an extract from 'French Revolution by Eric Hobsbawn from *New York Review* 22.5.69. Copyright © 1969 E.J. Hobsbawm; the proprietors of *Le Nouvel Observateur* for extracts from 'La Greve à la S.A.V.I.E.M.' by Lucien Rioux; 'Nanterre-la-Folie' by Yvon Le Vaillant, 'Reponse d'un oppresseur' by Maurice Merleau-Ponty, 'Notre Commune du 10 Mai' by D. Cohn-Bendit, 'Les Techniques des manifestations' by Rene Backmann, 'Les semeurs du desordre' by Katia D. Kaupp, 'L'Idee neuve de Mai 1968' by J.P. Sartre, 'L'heure de l'inventaire' by Jean Daniel; the proprietors of *The Observer* for extracts from an article on Referendum of 27.4.69. by Robert Stephens and John de St. Jorre from *The Observer* 27.4.69.; Penguin Books Ltd. for extracts from *French Revolution* by P. Seale and M. McConville; Stage 1 for extracts from *La Greve à Flins* by J.P. Talbo from May 1968: *The Renault Strike at Flins* copyright © Stage 1, 1970.; the proprietors of *The Times* for extracts from 'Teachers and Pupils take over Schools' 21.5.68., 'The French Students' by P. Brogan 18.6.69., and 'Achievements of Fifth Republic' by P. Brogan 30.5.68. from *The Times*.

For permission to reproduce copyright photographs we are grateful to the following: Associated Press, page 89 (top); J. Suquet-I.P.N. page 89 (bottom); United Press International, page 90.

Foreword

In the past, History traditionally has suffered as a subject from the distance placed between the student and the events themselves by the historian's own account—the interpretation of evidence in textbook, specialised account or article. This series is intended to supplement the account given by the historian with a presentation of the documents themselves so as to enable the student to form his own opinion based upon the evidence. This open-ended approach will allow the student to consider the material from which historical judgements are made and to examine critically the contemporary reaction to the events themselves.

Each contributor in the series will consider a major crisis in history and examine its complexities by means of selected documents and a short commentary. Each teacher is likely to have his own idea of how to make the best use of the material in each book. However, as an appendix to each volume, the author, while making no attempt to sum up, will suggest some of the problems which arise from the historical evidence within the documents. A full list of sources of documents appears in the Appendix to each volume, and where relevant a glossary is also given.

HARRY BROWNE
Series editor

Preface

There are not inconsiderable problems in attempting to give a reliable and balanced picture of any event so close to us as what occurred in France in May and June 1968. Even the terms which one might be tempted to apply could be misleading. To qualify it as a revolution, an insurrection, or a general strike, or to fall back on a formula such as a political crisis might be to make a judgment where none is yet possible. I have therefore called this book the May Events 1968 believing that this form of words, paradoxically preferred by both the Gaullists and the extreme Left who were parties to the conflict, is the least likely to prejudice the reader in advance of a careful consideration of the evidence.

The second and perhaps more formidable type of problem is presented by the difficulty of reconstructing what really happened in May 1968 in France. Not only was the movement unexpected, uncoordinated and uneven in every sense (geographical, political and social) but it did not create its own effective explanation, its own theory, for itself, nor did it find any ready-made model which explained it satisfactorily, although many were being offered. Those who took part in the events were also 'in the dark' and their proclaimed demands and conscious attempts to give a theoretical basis to their experience often betrayed the real sense of what was happening. This theoretical confusion applies equally to the policies and interpretations of the Government, the political parties and the trade unions. At the same time most of the would-be theorists are dogmatically convinced of the justice of their explanation. To understand the events in all their complexity would require a fundamental effort of 'theory' of a type not yet available in France, or perhaps in Britain. Had such a capacity to achieve genuine critical comprehension of what was happening existed, the events might have had a very different outcome.

Yet it is precisely because the existing political theory of western commentators on the events is so unsatisfactory and full of gaps that it is not too early to make an attempt at giving an objective account of the main events themselves and of the attitudes, fears and explanations which they evoked. The crisis is unresolved even today in France and the same crisis seems to be implicit in most western industrial countries. It is precisely because we do not yet understand and cannot adequately explain away the implications of the May events for all our lives, yet still suspect that their importance may be crucial, that the task of formulating an adequate theory must be faced. It may be that this kind of open-ended history, despite all the disadvantages of not being able to reach cut-and-dried and verifiable conclusions, provides one of the best forms of practical work for young historians today.

Introduction

The May 1968 Events in France were totally unexpected and quite unprecedented. That is perhaps their most remarkable feature. Almost all political scientists have long assumed that revolutions of the classical type will no longer happen in the economically advanced western countries, either because there is unlikely to be sufficient revolutionary discontent, or because such discontent is confined to fairly small marginal groups such as students and blacks, isolated from the rest of the people. Exceptions might be possible but none of them seemed to have much bearing on the situation in Western Europe. Least of all on France which until the beginning of May 1968 seemed to be at peace, rather successful in its international affairs, with a stable government, solid finances, and prosperity.

A revolution has never yet broken out under such circumstances. Yet in Paris in May 1968 it did. Or at least, something happened which might well have turned into a revolution.

In fact two things occurred which are remarkable, the second even more than the first: the students rebelled and forced the Government to retreat, and the workers followed their example.

Student rebellion is not uncommon these days. The novelty of the French situation of May 1968 lay in (a) success of the mass mobilisation of the students (not to mention their teachers and parents) and (b), the breadth of public support for them, which eventually forced the unions and the PCF, reluctantly, to line up behind them. In this situation there was not much the Government could do, short of starting to shoot; and it is much more difficult for a Government, even a Government as ready to resort to violence as the Gaullist Government had always been, to start a massacre of students than it is for it to shoot colonial subjects or even white workers. Nevertheless, nobody expected that the workers would imitate the students. What was quite new was that they did, uninfluenced by the obvious reluctance of the CGT and the PCF to become involved in a major tussle with the Government. It was the young workers who began the occupation of the factories which later snowballed into a general strike. The unions subsequently took over the leadership and organisation of the strike, but it remained an essentially spontaneous, grass-roots movement to the very end, and on several occasions the workers in the occupied factories dug in their heels and refused the terms negotiated on their behalf by their own leadership.

Subsequently there was a political crisis which shook the French establishment to its very roots. For a week the whole structure of Gaullist power seemed to be tottering. It was only saved in extremis by de Gaulle's fighting speech on 30 May.

Could it have happened anywhere else except in France? In the precise form that it took, it seems unlikely. In no other country is revolution so much a part of the national tradition, so that in certain circumstances large masses of people feel it is quite natural to put up a barricade or raise the red flag. The French workers may have been no more revolutionary in their practical demands than the British, but their ancestors for five generations back had made revolutions, and they had a bad conscience about not making one themselves. It was this factor that made it possible for the students, by their example, to make the working-class return to its traditions.

The object of this book is to give the essential background to the May Events, to narrate them in as lively a way as possible, and to illustrate them with the relevant documents. These illustrative documents may be eye-witness accounts or newspaper comment of various kinds. But in a situation where what is happening in the street is so closely related to the slogans and ideas of all parties involved, where words are as important and as dangerous as cobble-stones, a good deal of space must be given also to the statements of the protagonists, whether these came in the form of press communiqués, speeches in the street or in the National Assembly, broadcasts on radio or television, or simply slogans painted upon walls.

The general background to French politics and the particular history of student politics in France during the period immediately preceding the May Events is dealt with first. The main phases of the May Events themselves can be divided up as follows:

(a) the student revolt, at first limited to Nanterre, suddenly spreads to the whole of France and after the rioting culminating in the battle of the Rue Gay Lussac on 11 May and the general strike and demonstration of 13 May 1968, it leads to the general occupation of the Universities.

(b) Starting with the Sud-Aviation factory in Nantes, the strike movement (with occupation of the factories) spreads rapidly; by 17 May the union leaders are beginning to reassert their control and conclude the agreements of the Rue de Grenelle on 25 May;

(c) after rejection of the Grenelle agreements by the rank and file, the crisis moves into a political phase, the Left squabbling over the succession and the Gaullists in disarray until de Gaulle's broadcast of 30 May;

(d) the ebbing away of the revolutionary movement as the Gaullists regain courage and all the main parties accept the prospect of elections, while piecemeal agreements are negotiated by the unions; the election campaign and its results conclude the May Events.

Each of these phases represents a fresh aspect of the main crisis of the May Events. Each one in this book is narrated and documented separately for this reason.

Finally there is a brief section dealing with the consequences of the May Events in so far as they are discernible. In a real sense the sequel of the story has yet to unfold. It may well prove to be far more momentous than anything that has so far occurred, and far more widespread.

Background

'Revolutions are festivals of the oppressed and the exploited. . . . At such times the people are capable of performing miracles, if judged by the limited, philistine yardstick of gradualist progress. But it is essential that leaders of the revolutionary parties, too, should advance their aims more comprehensively and boldly at such a time, so that their slogans shall always be in advance of the revolutionary initiative of the masses, serve as a beacon . . . and show them the shortest and most direct route to complete, absolute and decisive victory. . . . '

V. I. Lenin:
Two Tactics of Social-Democracy, 1905.

1 · Antecedents of the Student Revolt

Chronology of Events

1946–68

The number of students entering university rises by over 400 per cent. There is no corresponding rise in staff and facilities—or in jobs for graduates.

1965

The creation of larger university-type units, combining hostels and faculties, brings about the formation of the student movement. The early debates and agitations of this movement concern the university hostels where the internal regulations are such as to keep the students, most of whom are living on insufficient grants, within the limitations of a semi-boarding school discipline. First electoral alliance between FGDS (Federation of the Left: main non-communist opposition group led by François Mitterrand), and PCF (French Communist Party) in Presidential Elections.

1966 January

The Caen Congress on reform of teaching. M. Fouchet, then Minister of Education: 'The dam will break if we do nothing'.

1967 March

A number of extreme revolutionary groups have an all-European meeting in Brussels: they analyse contemporary society and conclude that the contradictions of capitalism have now created a real possibility of revolutionary action. They set up a permanent secretariat to organise the campaign of protest against the war in Vietnam.

1967 October

In Strasbourg a meeting is held of the Ministers of Education of the six Common Market countries: the decisions taken concern examinations. They are not such as to give any satisfaction to militant students. Violent demonstrations of agricultural and industrial workers at Quimper and Le Mans.

1967 November

The Fouchet Plan is approved by the French Government: the education system is to become more responsive to the requirements of society and the economy by greater selectivity at all levels. The student movement is centred in Nanterre where a politically aware minority sees the Fouchet reform as a plan to 'enslave the university to the needs of industry'.

A committee of students and lecturers is set up at Nanterre in order to work out alternative proposals, but it has no practical results. At the Faculty of Sociology, Daniel Cohn-Bendit belonging to the anarchist group 'Red and Black' begins his political activity at this time. At Nanterre, the UEC (Communist Student Movement) remains outside the early struggles of the students and sometimes openly opposes them (as far back as January 1967 at its 28th Congress, the PCF spokesman Georges Marchais had defined the student agitation as the activity of 'small groups of young agitators not representing anything'). The luckless, liberal Rector of Nanterre, Grappin, initiates an attempt at disciplinary repression by drawing up blacklists, and plain clothes policemen begin to work within the university.

1968 January

Fearing clashes between extreme right-wing elements belonging to the Occident organisation and groups of left-wing students, the Rector calls in the police.

1968 February

Fighting in Caen between police and SAVIEM strikers and students. The students of various colleges throughout France occupy the female hostels; the police are called in to remove them. At Nantes 45 students are arrested. In Paris 2,000 students demonstrate against the Government's action in closing down the Cinémathèque Française: the Government sends in the police. On 22 February the Minister of Education, Peyrefitte, announces that there will be changes in the regulations of the university campuses. The reform, however, only concerns minimal domestic demands of the students, deliberately ignoring all the demands involving greater freedom of discussion and political organisation within the university world. Joint declaration of PCF and FGDS on progress towards a common electoral platform for the Left.

1968 March

15–17 March.   At Amiens a debate is held on the reform of teaching; the slogan is 'Learn to teach'.
17–18 March.   During the night, bombs are thrown at two American banks and offices of three American firms.
17 March.   UNEF (main French Union of Students) conference disrupted by Trotskyite students.
20 March.   The windows of the 'American Express' office in Paris are smashed. Six people arrested, including a student from Nanterre.
21 March.   Peyrefitte should address the new Faculty of Science. A large number of students gather at the Halles aux Vins (Faculty annexe) and the Minister prefers to avoid an encounter with them. The students form a procession and march to the Ministry of Education. At Bordeaux and in Nantes the agitation continues. Student protests in Dijon.
22 March.   At Nanterre 142 students occupy the administrative block in protest at arrests of students. Trotskyite, Maoist, and Anarchist groups merge into a single group, the Mouvement du 22 mars, one of whose promoters is Daniel Cohn-Bendit. The programme of this group is to 'oppose a future as watchdogs, to oppose exams and degrees which reward those who cooperate in the system'.
28 March.   The UNEF calls a demonstration and demands the building of new university premises in the Parisian region. The UEC holds a conference at which the 'anarchism' of Nanterre is denounced. New debates are organised at Nanterre on the subjects: 'Capitalism in 1968 and the struggles of the working class', 'The critical university', 'The anti-imperial struggle'. Grappin suspends lectures for two days.
The students take no notice and hold a meeting in front of the university buildings; only the Communist students fail to attend. Peyrefitte on TV: 'The hotheads among the students are discrediting them-

1968 April

selves with their fellows because of their own excesses.'

The faculty at Nanterre is re-opened and lecture hall B, officially given over to the students for holding their meetings, is re-named by them the 'Che Guevara Hall'.

11 April.   Attempted assassination of Rudi Dutschke (German student leader) in Berlin.

20 April.   A solidarity demonstration for Rudi Dutschke brings 2,000 students out to march through the Quartier Latin.

21 April.   At the UNEF conference the President is forced to resign by the extreme Left and the Vice-President Jacques Sauvageot, a PSU militant, is left in charge.

22 April.   The Cinémathèque Française reopens after the campaign carried on by the film-makers and students.

A demonstration of 'support for the Vietnamese people', organized by the UEC, brings 5,000 students out in a peaceful march through the Quartier Latin.

25 April.   Students of the Maison du Portugal in the Cité Universitaire in Paris invade and smash up the American hostel.

26 April.   Pierre Juquin, Communist MP, who had been invited to speak in the Che Guevara lecture hall at Nanterre, is thrown out by Maoist students; Laurent Schwartz, the PSU (a small extreme-left Socialist Party) speaker, is shouted down. Members of the Occident movement throw a smoke bomb and two ink bombs into the UNEF headquarters.

2 · Background to the Student Unrest

1 · The Student Crisis in France

The background to the discontent, and ultimately the rebellion, of the French students is well summarised in this article by Nesta Roberts.

'The Guardian',
22 February 1968

Students at the University of Nantes last week invaded the rector's quarters, tearing down curtains and scattering books and papers. They were dispersed by the police after a brisk exchange of blows, stones, and tear-gas bombs.

Students at the university residence of Bures-sur-Yvette (Essonne) last spring subjected their director to a campaign of persecution, ranging from letting down the tyres of his car to breaking the windows of his office, which led to his offering his resignation.

Students at the vast 'University City' of Antony, in the suburbs of Paris, in October, 1965, staged riots which it took a force of several hundred police to quell.

In each instance they were demonstrating against what they consider to be the childish and unreasonable system of discipline imposed in university halls of residence. It is a long-standing grievance which the Minister of Education, M. Alain Peyrefitte, will be recognising today when he announces a reform which should 'modify the conditions of life for students in the residencies.' If students are so far inclined to be sceptical about its effects, it is perhaps because the Minister

went on to say that the new measures would 'attempt to reconcile the aspirations for a broadening of the regulations with the exigencies imposed by the organisation of their work and the moral responsibility of the public authority.' (The last is a reference to the fact that, under French law, every minor living in a boarding establishment away from his family is placed under the protection of the authorities.) M. Peyrefitte is on record also as saying that university residencies are 'essentially places of work.'

Specifically, during the action campaign which opened last week, the students are protesting against a list of interdictions which recalls a seaside boarding house or the more unfortunate women's training colleges in Britain ten years or so ago. Men and women students may not visit each other's rooms freely, they may not receive in their rooms any visitors from outside (occasionally this applies even to relatives), they may not imprint their individual personality on their rooms to the extent of driving in a nail to hang a picture, they may not indulge in any kind of propaganda on the premises, and all notices, posters, or invitations to visiting speakers must first be vetted by the director. Basically the rules were taken over from those framed for the 'internat'

(boarding department) of lycées at a time when the religious and political neutrality of State education was the subject of fanatical attention.

Hence the strictures against propaganda: hence, too, the prohibition of pin-ups or even Picasso prints. It is possible to circumnavigate them. At Antony, since the violence in 1965, a liberal and relatively youthful director has instituted a regime, involving fortnightly meetings of a management committee on which staff and students are equally represented, which has brought peace and reason to a notorious trouble spot. This is an exception. Talk to residents of other halls and you hear that 'we are there only to work and eat and sleep,' or that 'we cannot choose our own recreation,' or that 'we were not allowed to have a meeting of information about Vietnam because it was political, but when General Beaufre came to talk about nuclear strategy that wasn't political, so it was allowed.'

To say that the persistent unrest of the past few years is not really about these things is not to suggest that the present complaints are unjustified. For the most part they are justified, and to meet them would certainly bring a modicum of domestic calm and wellbeing, but in itself it would not dissipate the mood of anger and sometimes bewildered bloody-mindedness, as of badly led trade unionists, or an unhappy ship's company, or a regiment whose morale has slumped, which is evident among students. They talk, with a sincerity not impaired by the jargon in which it tends to be clothed, about paternalism of the less imaginative sort, and about segregation from the problems of the world which they are soon to enter, and about the the liaison between the structure and content of the university course and the present political set-up.

'They make statements without demonstrating them to be true.' 'They tell us Marx is old hat.' 'In the psychosociology course Freud is ignored or his teaching is distorted.' Ask: 'What exactly do you mean by that?' at almost any point during the catalogue and the answer may be rather approximate, but there is no mistaking the message. It speaks of resentment at being treated like schoolboys, of almost total absence of dialogue between students and authority, of the students' feeling that they have no say in the direction of their own lives.

Given today's physical conditions, the unease is inevitable. France's tradition of free entry to the university for every holder of the baccalaureate certificate is no more adapted to the enormous post-war expansion both of population and of secondary education, than are existing buildings and staff to the invading hordes of bacheliers, and these are not deficiencies that can be made good rapidly. Growth rates are uneven. Professors are drawn from the holders of doctorates, and the number of doctorates in the humanities gained during 1965 was little larger than the number gained during 1913, whereas the number of students showed, by contrast, an astronomical progression.

At the beginning of the present academic year there were 514,000 university students in France, 56,000 more than the previous year. Paris had 156,000. How much staff-student contact can take place when groups for practical work number as many as forty?

Necessarily the expansion, even had it been less sensational, would have involved decent-ralisation, and France, since the war, has adopted the principle of the campus for its university extensions. Twelve per cent of today's student population is so lodged, and it is planned that in ten years or so, almost half will be. This comes at a time when there are signs that students in general no longer wish to be isolated from the world, and in a country which has no strong tradition of and, it might be thought, no very marked gift for corporate life. Even so, the campus idea might have been made acceptable, but the present 'cités universitaires' are not yet campuses. For the most part they are barracks.

Underlying it all is a failure rate which is the world's highest. M. Peyrefitte has himself acknowledged and deplored the fact. There are certain faculties where only one student in four graduates.

The Minister, speaking at Besançon last year, found a telling phrase to describe the existing situation: 'It is as if we organised a shipwreck in order to pick out the best swimmers, who would be the only ones to escape drowning.'

2 · The folly of Nanterre

'Le Nouvel Observateur,'
21 February 1968

One day, at a Cabinet meeting, a discussion was going on about the need to create a new campus outside Paris to cope with the growing influx of new students. Certainly, but where? M. Messmer, Minister of the Armed Forces, said to his colleague, M. Fouchet, then Minister of Education: 'I have a bit of military land to the west of Paris, down Nanterre way. You could use it if you like.' That was some years ago. Today the 'little bit of military land', formerly an air force dump, has become the 'university complex' of Nanterre, which will perhaps remain as a monument to one of the greatest follies of the de Gaulle epic.

Seen from outside, from the council flats which jostle it and the shanty towns rotting at its feet, this model university seems like an enclosure of privilege, a dazzling but provocative shop-window in which the spoilt children of the rich parade. But the awful truth is that the inhabitants of the shanty towns and of the council blocks are so used to class injustice that when they are asked about it they reply that they have not got any opinions on the matter, that it is none of their business, that they do not give a damn.

A sociologist has told me: 'Nanterre is the folly of just about everybody', the folly of those who were in the first place responsible for its building, the folly of its surroundings, the folly of the town planners.... Gleaming blocks of plate glass and concrete, standing in the mud of a waste lot. The décor does not encourage enthusiasm and living in it is not conducive to peace of mind. First of all you get bored, especially for the students who live in. There is not much to do. Twice a week there is the cinema club and now and then a poetry reading, a jazz concert, a dance. Most people watch the telly. The telly is an opiate. You go into the cafeteria, but it is only open at odd hours. You can go in two or three little bistros outside and especially to one called the Faculté which is linked directly to the hostel by a muddy little lane. This Faculty bistro is the great place for philosophical, political discussions, for love affairs and the pin ball table. But it is closed on Sundays. Just like the cafeteria.

Nobody really knows anybody else but gossip is rife. This closed-in life of course brings on crises of boredom and nervous depression.

Add to all that the feeling, which is very depressing for young people, of still being treated as children, just at the time when they would like to enjoy their new-found liberty. When they are asked which they would choose, further development of cultural activity on the campus, or more personal liberty, they reply: liberty. The students find the regulations of the campus humiliating and hypocritical. They are at the very least out of date: the students have no more rights than pupils at boarding schools: no girls allowed in the bedrooms; no changes of any sort to be made to the accommodation, no moving furniture,

no hooks or nails to be put into the walls; no meals to be prepared in the bedrooms; no political or religious propaganda to be carried on anywhere inside the hostel, etc. One student showed me his bedroom and said: 'I'm breaking at least nine rules in here'.

At the Faculty, it is the sociologists who are both the spearhead and the catalyst. A few hundred students, four lecturers and a dozen assistant lecturers have set up a kind of 'soviet' here. The demands are not of the same kind as at hostels, although there is a link. They concern the whole conception of the university.

What kind of university shall we have tomorrow? The students wish to participate in working this out. What is striking at Nanterre, is the leading role played by the Anarchists and by groups of those demanding 'joint management'.

This latter tendency has been dominant since November, led by the Trotskyists and the militant Catholics who were demanding an increased participation of the students in the decisions and organisation of the universities themselves. At Nanterre departmental assemblies have been set up and monthly discussions organised between pupils and lecturers. The only assembly which really works is that in the Department of Sociology. For in the old departments, dialogue is difficult.

A lecturer told me: 'The crisis in the university is extraordinarily grave. The universities in France and throughout Europe are completely out of date. The great risk is that people will not understand the importance of the problems which we are facing and that they will imagine that everything can be settled by introducing a few new rules'. What some of the students are now criticising radically is not just the structure of the

university but also the form and content of teaching. They are fighting against the old image of the lecturer-father, the sole depositary of a truth which it is his task to transmit from where he sits on high in his professorial chair. They want courses to be something other than séances in which the students passively ingest anything that is handed out. They want, for example, all the ideologies taught in the departments to be open to criticism by the students. In a word: they want to provoke an upheaval in the traditional forms of teacher-student relationship.

In the course of a few months dialogue has turned into conflict and then into breakdown of relations. This means the failure of a certain type of paternalism. At present there are several bones of contention. First of all, the business of the 'blacklist' (of 'subversive' students). Much ink has been flowing about this. Despite all the communiqués, no one can say whether such a list ever existed. A well-known Nanterre lecturer stated that it did at an extremely official meeting. The Dean immediately became indignant, the Dean is an honourable man. So is the lecturer.

Then there is the business of the plain-clothes policemen. They have been seen on the premises, they have been photographed. But where do they come from? And on whose orders? The administration's? or the Central Intelligence Agency?

Finally, the 'Cohn-Bendit affair'. When the Minister for Youth and Sport, M. François Missoffe, came to inaugurate the swimming pool (the students would have preferred a library), Dany Cohn-Bendit, 22, a brilliant but turbulent troublemaker belonging to the Anarchist group, pointed out to him that in his white paper he did not make any reference to the sexual problems of students. Missoffe ended up by telling him that if he needed to work off steam he could go and take a dive into the pool. It was then that Cohn-Bendit talked about 'Hitlerism'. Since then he has written to Missoffe, to apologise, not for what he said but for the way he said it. Missoffe replied that he had forgotten everything.

Are these just isolated inci- dents? Last Sunday I was talking to a dozen students belonging to the UNEF in a little room on whose walls were slogans and a hammer and sickle. (There are slogans written up everywhere; in a lift I read 'Alcohol kills, Kiss a girl, Take LSD', 'Long live the revolt of the Saigon workers', 'All reactionaries are paper tigers'.) The UNEF students told me: 'The administration has managed to make the whole thing into a series of isolated incidents. In fact every- thing must be seen in a single con- text: the repression of all and any movement which might contest society and the present régime.' For them, their struggle and the ensuing repression are of the same kind as that of the workers of the factories on strike at Caen.

3 · Statistical table showing social discrimination in French University entrance pattern

The chances of obtaining a university education in France are shown in the following table

Social class of student's parents	Per cent of total population	Per cent of University entry in 1964
1 Professions and senior managerial	4.0	58.5
2 Junior managerial	7.8	29.6
3 Employers and self-employed	10.4	16.4
4 Office workers	12.6	9.5
5 Peasant farmers	15.7	3.6
6 Service staff	5.4	2.4
7 Industrial workers	36.7	1.4
8 Agricultural labourers	4.3	0.7

Note that the upper middle class, 1, has well over half the places at University although it numbers less than a twentieth of the population. Conversely the working class, 7 and 8, though almost half the population, has only 2 per cent of the places at University. This clearly illustrates the way in which the French school-system acts as a social barrier. Only about half the students in French Universities (before 1968) finished their courses and obtained degrees. (The success rate in Britain is over 90 per cent.)

4 · Manifesto on education drawn up by the student rebels

This manifesto illustrates the radical approach to their own and others' learning problems adopted by the student rebels.

Article 1   All those who possess knowledge, who possess education, are required to 'hand back' as individuals what they have received as a privilege from society, in order that knowledge may in future no longer be a privilege.
Article 2   It is decreed that education from now on should be permanent, free, and obligatory at all ages.
Article 3   All those who have had a higher education are called upon to offer to others the benefit of the advantage they have

acquired by it. All students must become teachers while continuing to be students.

Article 4   Any former teacher must fulfil his teaching duties, to which is added that of training his new colleagues.

Article 5   All workers are required, having until today been deprived of 'knowledge' and whatever their level of education, and age, to become 'learners,' and subsequently teachers in order to be able to choose their own destiny.

Article 6   Any local educational unit (factories, former elementary schools, former secondary schools, former colleges) will be administered by the whole body of the workers/teachers/students attending it.

Article 7   All workers/teachers/students will be elected, dismissed or promoted by their peers, and the decisions will be taken by a simple majority.

Article 8   From now on, there will be no professors. The problem of the shortage of professors is resolved, since any person who has been taught will give back in the form of training and teaching in the same measure as he has learned, naturally at the level of his competence.

Article 9   Formal examinations will no longer be necessary since knowledge will be checked continuously.

Article 10   For each economic, political or cultural unit of production and consumption of both 'goods' and 'culture' an elected commission will take all decisions. This commission will be subject to recall by a simple majority vote of no confidence.

5 · Response of an orthodox professor to student reform proposals

Typical of the 'orthodox' response to student radicalism about the form and content of University courses is this excerpt from an article by the Professor of Epistemology at Nanterre.

**'Le Nouvel Observateur',
13 March 1968**

Some of the bolder spirits seem to be reasoning basically as follows: the university forms the cadres of society; if these cadres are taught, firstly nothing, secondly to deny everything that other people say, and everything that they say themselves, the fish will rot and perish from the head down; in certain leaflets, they talk about the 'paralysis' then of the 'destruction' of the university. This is very well thought out and very well put; it will take us back to the Stone Age quicker than the atom bomb and napalm perhaps. In my youth, Nizan used to denounce the 'watchdogs', but all those who regarded themselves as 'revolutionaries' knew and said that ignorance and stupidity play the game of reaction. Our modern revolutionaries have revolutionised all that. The less well-endowed, who are no doubt the majority, probably simply enjoy the debates, the dialogues (if they are peaceful), the contestations (if they are aggressive), where people say what they like, and words are inflated and made brilliantly amusing with the give and take of the discussion; it is so much easier to give one's opinions and to 'contest' than to listen to a lecture. Than to prepare one too ... We lecturers are also inclined to go running off too often to colloquiums and conversations, we too take too much delight in the nothingness of 'exchanges of views' for us to have the right to be astonished that our students dream of these games which they are half-forbidden to play themselves.

So everybody should get back to work! It is up to us lecturers to say it and to be the first to do it.

6 · Occident anti-militant leaflet

The extreme Right response to the growing activities of the student militants is reflected in the text of this leaflet distributed in April 1968 by the Occident movement.

Young French people are tired:

Of being constantly given pamphlets in favour of the Vietcong assassins at the doors of their places of work, their faculties and their schools.

Of seeing the eternal traitors who only yesterday were supporting the Vietminh torturers and Arab terrorists in the name of 'PEACE', today becoming the hirelings of the Vietcong.

These people have tried the patience of French youth for too long and they know it. For more than fifteen days now, agents in the pay of Hanoi who come to distribute their calls to treason have regularly been put to flight by schoolboys and students united under the French nationalists.

The OCCIDENT movement spearheads this opposition. For several years now it has been fighting against the physical and moral terrorism used by the reds against French Youth in the name of their 'liberty'.

The OCCIDENT movement has been able, by virtue of its activities, its posters and its demonstrations, to get the upper hand in the street and make the marxists understand that their dictatorship has come to an end.

Join OCCIDENT and fight against reaction and the red front by fighting for a People's National Regime.

THE NATIONALIST YOUTH MOVEMENT

3 · Background to Industrial Unrest

7 · Economic balance-sheet of ten years of Gaullism

'The Economist',
18 May 1968

Ten years ago this month General de Gaulle swept into power amid the pentasyllabic chants from the Right of 'Algérie française,' and from the Left of 'la girafe au zoo.' Since then France has prospered mightily, under a government which has followed almost precisely the opposite policy to that which was originally intimated as its objective.

A main key to its economic advance was a 14.93 per cent devaluation at the end of 1958, which was at first criticised by all the experts as being unaccompanied by sufficient measures of internal restraint; but which, after two months of a hectic consumer spree at the beginning of 1959, then moved into a period of almost magical success, so that conventional economists and international central bankers have been fibbing ever since that they always recognised it to be a model sort of devaluation in the first place. Or, almost ever since. From the middle of 1963 on, France's economic record has been less brilliant, so that now whispers have begun to be heard that, just as Britain in 1959, ten years after its first devaluation, swept a government into power on a slogan of 'never had it so good' while actually the woodworm was already gnawing in the panelling, so France reaches this tenth anniversary of the gaul-list coup with perhaps, after all. . . .

The core of the problem—and of the achievement—can be fairly simply stated, although it rather rarely is. By comparison with sister nations like Britain or Germany, France's resources—and particularly its workers—are still grossly maldistributed between occupations. About 17 per cent of its labour force is still in agriculture, where productivity per worker is less than half the average in the rest of the French economy. Even outside agriculture, France has twice as many people listed as self-employed or unpaid family workers as Britain has, many of them in France's terrible, antiquated, small shopkeeper, retail trade with very low productivity. Only about 28 per cent of France's working population (against over 35 per cent of both Britain's and Germany's) is in manufacturing, and quite a lot even of this is carried on in impossibly small factories, often situated in villages or very small towns. Remarkably, France is still a country where nearly 50 per cent of the population lives in communes of less than 2,000 inhabitants. It is a country with more than twice the land area of either Britain or West Germany, but a population (which last year went over the 50 million mark) still slightly smaller than either of them.

Yet this maldistributed labour force, this community which one might suspect from the population statistics of being half composed of rural bumpkins and hicks, manages to produce an average internal income per head which is broadly equivalent to Britain's: by some measurements—those quoted by General de Gaulle in his speeches—slightly higher, by others slightly behind. The average Frenchman eats and drinks better than the average Englishman (over 15 per cent more carcase meat), and is more likely to have a car (214 per thousand of population last year versus Britain's 178). Against that, the Englishman has a much better-appointed and roomier main dwelling place (although more of the French urban middle class will have in addition a weekend cottage at the seaside or in the country), and the English have considerably more domestic consumer durables such as television sets and telephones. The general impression that Britain is still a rather richer country is confirmed by such figures as those of infant mortality (four per thousand more French babies die) and the much higher figures for British (and German) consumption of energy per head, although these are partly a reflection of the more rural flavour of French society. In quality of urban life, there is not very much in it. France's national income is clearly some billions of francs higher than one would expect it to be, after seeing how its workers are deployed.

8 · Employers' attitudes and the economic situation in spring 1968
(Gretton)

The French industrial revolution started later, took longer, and even now is less complete than in most other Western industrialised countries. Even today it is not uncommon in the provinces to find small and medium-sized firms whose managerial staff is recruited entirely through relations and marriage alliances, to whom the term 'market research' refers to something the wife or the maid does once a week, and who employ the familiar and degrading *tu* to men who are expected to reply with *vous* and *Monsieur*.

Further, the Patronat have succeeded in imposing the 'département' as the level at which wage negotiations take place for any one sector of industry (e.g. metalworkers, including both automobile and steel workers, and building workers). This avoids the inconvenience of national agreements, as in Sweden or Britain, that it is difficult to escape implementing them; it also avoids the obvious danger of plant agreements, such as are common in the United States, of dividing the Patronat against itself. It is significant that very few followed Renault's courageous initiative in signing a plant agreement in 1954, and of those that did fewer and fewer renewed them.

But the fundamental objection to plant agreements is that they look far too much like some form of 'participation'. For it is obviously unrealistic to expect employer and union to negotiate seriously if the latter cannot look at the books. Even if the former resorted to cooking up yet another set of crooked ones (there is already one for tax purposes), the very principle is something that the Patronat will never willingly admit.

As for the general economic situation, in the spring of 1968 it was causing anxiety to the Government, employers and workers. A balance of payments problem had begun to appear for the first time for several years, production was stagnant, investment at a minimum, and the Bourse even less active than usual (at the best of times it plays nothing like the same role as the London or New York stock exchanges, as Frenchmen tend to consider it only as a source of quick profits, and look to the State, property or their mattresses to safeguard their long-term savings), so that at the beginning of the year the Government was forced to take some measures to encourage consumer spending. The imminent end of protectionism within the Common Market had caused a veritable panic among employers; in 1966 there were more mergers than in the whole of the previous decade, and there were as many as 60 in 1967 alone (still fewer than in Britain, however). And, for the workers, there was unemployment. For although official statistics on the subject are notoriously inaccurate, it is generally agreed that the figure of 500,000 was reached before the strike broke out. The most alarming aspect of this, although in view of the demographic situation not the most surprising, was the number of young people affected. It was still easy to find work at apprentice rates, but once they reached the age of eighteen a great many could not find any job at all, or at best one well below their qualifications.

9 · Workers, employers and unions
(Seale and McConville)

The background to the second phase of the Events was the simmering unrest in French industry, compounded of unemployment, low wages, a dictatorial attitude among employers and the inadequacy of the trade unions to bargain effectively.

First was the crude fact that minimum wages in France were scandalously low, and that, in the ten years of Gaullist rule, the gap between workers' incomes and those of the managerial class had widened. This prosperity, of which they had little part, could no longer be hidden from the workers: it was rammed down their throats by television and by increasingly pervasive advertising vaunting the *dolce vita* of a consumer society. Before the May–June wage settlements, a quarter of all French wage-earners earned less than 550 francs a month (about £46) and a third earned less than 720 francs (£60); about one and a half million wage-earners on the very bottom of the scale—unskilled industrial workers and agricultural labourers—made little more than 400 francs a month (about £33). For much of this underprivileged population hourly rates had fallen well behind those of France's Common Market partners (except Italy), and only heavy overtime allowed many workers to climb above subsistence level. These abysmal figures are only part of the picture. By May 1968 French unemployment had soared to over 500,000, hitting not only depressed areas, as in many other industrial countries caught in a process of transformation, but particularly the young. In Burgundy, for instance, home of the Socialist leader François Mitterand, 29 per cent of young people under 25 were unemployed.

The situation inside many French factories is positively medieval by British or American standards. Companies like Michelin used to boast that they had talked to strikers only three times in thirty years. Peugeot last June called in the riot police to clear their factories and, in the skirmishes, two men were killed. Citroën, another prominent French car manufacturer, has a reputation among workers for running a penitentiary rather than a factory. Union rights in its plants are negligible. Men of different nationality—Algerians, Yugoslavs, Spaniards—are often placed side by side on the production line to cut out talking. One third of the workers in Citroën's Paris plants are immigrants housed in company hostels. Thousands more of these foreign workers—particularly Spanish and Portuguese—are employed in big French engineering firms. Indeed it could be argued that the influx of foreign labour into France over the past decade has strengthened the employers' position, and has been an important brake on union militancy. Nothing could match the joy and sense of liberation with which the Citroën plants were 'occupied'.

Not all companies are as repressive as Citroën, but most are traditionally secretive and paternalistic. Their published accounts are virtually meaningless. Workers are told little of management plans, production targets, or possible short-time working. This secrecy extends to lower managerial levels, which may be one reason why the great majority of skilled men and supervisory grades strongly backed the May–June strike.

These nineteenth century conditions have survived in France in part because French unions have not been able to put up much of a fight since the Second World War. The explanation is complex, but it has something to do with the fact that the Communist-led CGT has shied away from anything that might seem like treasonable collaboration with the capitalist enemy. The CGT focused its attention on wage levels, disdaining involvement in corporate affairs, a guaranteed working week, a minimum monthly wage—let alone the formation of works councils. To show an interest in them would be an acknowledgement that private capitalism was here to stay. This CGT attitude suited a large number of older French workers who still had roots in the land. They wished to have nothing to do with French industrial capitalism except to draw money from it.

But a new generation is growing up which finds inadequate this view of a union's role. It believes workers' representatives should be involved in decision-making at plant level; it is deeply concerned with the recognition of union rights and the spread of information from the manager's office downwards. These ideas have found a champion in the CFDT which, although now independent of the Catholic Church, remains permeated with the radical philosophy of French left-wing Catholicism. Here is at least one source for the view, heard constantly among workers during May, that work is more than money and that human dignity is as valid a union claim as a bigger pay packet.

To summarize what is a complex and constantly moving subject, the CGT is wage-orientated, while the CFDT seeks profound reforms at the factory level to give the workers a direct share in management. What was striking about the May crisis is that it saw the emergence of yet a third trend on the French labour scene, as hostile to the CFDT as to the CGT. This trend was frankly revolutionary: its ambition to overthrow capitalism led it first to attempt to undermine the Communist-led CGT monolith, which it saw as an unwitting pillar of the bourgeois state.

10 · Union demands in spring 1968

'L'Express',
15 April 1968
**The Battle of the Ten
Thousand Hours**

Of all the industrial countries, France, despite its four weeks of paid holidays and its ten days of Bank Holidays, is the only one, apart from Japan, in which the working day has not gone down in ten years. The trade unions would like to reverse this tendency. They put forward three arguments:

Working conditions are becoming more and more difficult, and production line speeds have risen steadily.

Elevation of productivity ought to be of benefit to the worker. 'In 1945, say the unions, it took 3,600 man-hours to build a three-room apartment. In 1968 only one third of the man-hours were required for the same job. The workers should benefit from this progress.'

The reduction of working hours could make a contribution to

lowering unemployment.

On this particular front of their demands, the union headquarters have marked up several local successes.

But the battle is not yet really engaged. The two parties are sizing each other up and laying in a stock of arguments. On the employers' side, the resistance is considerable. 'Such measures, they say, will inevitably involve additional costs which our income and the foreign competition do not enable us to afford.' Reduction of the working week from 48 to 42 hours is the equivalent to an increase in salary of about 14 per cent.

Those most directly concerned, the wage-earners, seem, according to various surveys, to prefer an increase in their take-home pay to a reduction in working hours. In 50 years of active life, the average Frenchman works about 110,000 hours. He has the choice: he can chop off 10,000 hours from this total or change his car more often and get a bigger house. The choice is clear. But it is not simple.

11 · The strike at the SAVIEM lorry factory at Caen

'Le Nouvel Observateur', 13 February 1968

Last Monday, after an 11-day strike, the bitterest which has ever been seen in the Caen area, the 4,800 workers at the SAVIEM lorry factory started work again. At first, nobody was expecting the violence which twice was a feature of this conflict.

It began on 23rd January in a trivial way: the hours of work at the SAVIEM had been cut and the unions were claiming a rise of 6 per cent in order to make up for the fall in wages; but the management refused and declared that it could only give 2 per cent. So the strike was unleashed. Caen has the reputation of being a calm city, the workers have never shown much sign of belligerence and therefore it was thought that the strike would be a 'peaceful' one. However, the strike got steadily more bitter: first because of the attitude of the police, and then because of the participation of large numbers of young people.

The Prefect of police of the Calvados region, M. Portel, is a 'strong man'. When the strike was announced, he brought hundreds of CRS and mobile police to Caen. On Wednesday 24 January, a meeting of the strikers turned into a march to the town centre; the Prefect gave the order to stop it. There were clashes between policemen and strikers: and 15 people were hurt. Tension was mounting.

On Friday 26th at 6.30 pm a meeting was held in Caen. Numerous police surrounded the 8,000 workers of the SAVIEM and those from other firms which had also decided to go out on strike. About 7 pm, the demonstrators were on the point of dispersing when the order was given to the police to clear the square. They charged in immediately with rare energy, using the butts of their rifles and their long truncheons and throwing blast grenades. The workers hit back: bolts, stones and molotov cocktails rained down on the forces of law and order. The battle went on for four hours. The final balance-sheet: 100 wounded, 100 people arrested and beaten up by the police. On Sunday and Monday, the Lower Court which heard the cases handed down a dozen sentences of between 15 days and 3 months in prison, with or without probation. So much for the intervention of the police.

Now, let us look at the strikers. The SAVIEM company is an enterprise which has been operating in this area since 1962. Its staff are on average 25 years old. The young people who work at the factory are mostly tradesmen and have passed their appropriate technical exams. They entered the SAVIEM company precisely because it is one of the few companies of any importance in the region. They are employed there as skilled craftsmen but poorly paid (450 francs per month for a woman, 650 francs for a man) and working in extremely bad conditions. They have the feeling that their apprenticeship has been no value to them and that they have no future. They are disillusioned and bitter and not at all inclined to get knocked about without hitting back.

In the demonstrations, other young malcontents came and joined them: unemployed men (many of the 4,000 unemployed in the area are under 20 years old,) and the students from the University of Caen. The day of the demonstration at Caen, there were demonstrations in Lyon, Bordeaux, Marseille and other cities. But there were no incidents. At Caen, the Prefect was a man of order and he had no intention of 'leaving the streets to the workers'. He won. But one doesn't know for how long.

12 · The peasant revolt, October 1967

'L'Express', 9 October 1967

At nine o'clock in the evening last Monday, Quimper is a dead town; the ambulances leaving the prefecture skid on the nuts and bolts, and the fragments of glass which are littering the square. Victor Talbourdet, aged 32, three children, owner of fifty hectares in the Côtes du Nord district, is lying in a coma at the Morvan hospital in Brest.

In four hours the little town where happy holiday-makers go to try the oysters in mid-summer has become the symbol of one of the most dramatic problems in the changing state of France. The peasants condemned in their very livelihood by the economists and by 'the nature of things' have switched on a warning signal which the planners did not foresee: violence.

There were seven thousand peasants according to the prefecture, fifteen thousand according to the organisers of the demonstration. The meeting opens at the fairground at half past two. M. Andre Blejean shouts into the microphone: 'Twenty years ago, the price of pork was 262 francs a kilo, and that's what it still is. And that's our problem.'

The crowd shouts. Placards are raised: 'Che Guevara in Brittany', 'Brittany first, Quebec later'. The majority of the young men have motor-cycle helmets on their heads and iron bars and empty beer bottles in the pockets of their anoraks.

In front of the prefecture the battle begins at once. Stones, empty bottles, pieces of wood, then pieces of the road and cobbles torn up from the forecourt of the cathedral are all used as ammunition. Traffic signs, the flower stalls and boxes of flowers get thrown into the river. About seven o'clock in the evening, the battle pauses. After negotiations the leaders of the demonstration have decided to call a halt and the Prefect has agreed to release the seven demonstrators arrested during the riot. Balance-sheet: 179 police, and 80 demonstrators wounded.

On Tuesday morning, France is wondering what has happened. Why?

General de Gaulle himself asks this question to M. Edgar Faure at the special cabinet meeting the same day: 'Well, Mr Minister? They are demonstrating and they are setting fire to buildings. What do they want?'

The Fifth Republic has given to the farmer 3.7 milliard francs in 1958, 9.9 milliard in 1966. It is a considerable sum.

If half these amounts had been used for a real reconversion of agriculture, the drama of Quimper would perhaps have been avoided. But nobody dared to do it. The Government yielded to the peasants' insistence that they needed special crutches to limp in their own way.

Today, reality takes its revenge.

Becoming an industrial nation has to be paid for. The peasants of Quimper just reminded the whole of France of this. If the farmers follow their own slogans, then traditional unionism will be swept along on the tide. One of the leaders of the union has already predicted that if the Government does nothing then less reasonable people will replace the present leadership.

This time nobody dares guess what will happen: enquiries by the Prefects and public opinion polls are not capable of measuring the degree of anger which is hidden beneath the cottage roofs of forgotten France.

4 · Background to French Politics

The Historical Pattern

One of the most remarkable aspects of the May Events was the way it made all existing political formations and habits look irrelevant. There seemed to be little or no connection between what the party spokesmen were saying and what was actually happening in the country, and in the minds of its people. Even during the election campaign in June 1968, the main issues had very little to do with what had caused the riots and strikes. Nevertheless the old patterns were not swept away, the old parties fought the election, and that process itself did much towards restoring calm in the country, even if it solved no problems.

Since 1789 France has had 15 different constitutions, including 3 Empires and five Republics, with a continual alternation between weakly inefficient governments and ruthless and centralising ones. For the individual Frenchman, the Government is always to be regarded with suspicion, as a hostile and disrupting force in his life; for politicians, on the other hand, the people must, by force or guile, be ruled despite themselves. Historically, from Napoleon I down to de Gaulle, force has usually been preferred.

In such a prevailing climate there seems to be little scope for political parties, and as recently as 1962 a poll revealed that 49 per cent of people in France felt that no party genuinely represented their interests, despite the wide choice. Under the Third Republic, however, a system of parties, all of them claiming to embody the true heritage of the French Revolution, did develop, and the major issues of national life were debated and decided in a parliamentary context. Yet, divorced from their electors, except where local issues were concerned, deputies were free to manoeuvre for patronage and power in a way that accentuated rather than diminished the gap between Government and governed.

Between the wars voting patterns remained very stable (even the Popular Front of 1936 was elected as the result of a 1.5 per cent swing) and repeatedly threw up left of centre majorities which, when elections came round again four years later, had always become right of centre coalition governments in an endless series of re-shuffles. In 1940 and in 1958 when there was total disenchantment with this process and the consequent inability of French governments to deal with threats to national existence (the German invasion and the revolt of the Algerian colonists and regular army), the French accepted with relief the disappearance of the system and the emergence of a figurehead who would take responsibility for unwelcome decisions. After the Liberation the constitution of the Fourth Republic was not different enough from that of the Third to prevent the same pattern of democratic chaos from recurring. Parliamentary coalitions were unable to carry through the painful decolonisation and modernisation of industry without which France could not survive in Europe or the world. Although the record of the Fourth Republic is very good, in terms of post-war recovery and the creation of a second industrial revolution, the persistence of social and political attitudes and traditions which made it impossible for Governments to act decisively in moments of crisis made its overthrow inevitable.

The Fifth Republic has not changed the situation in any fundamental way. Parties are relatively unimportant and constantly change their principles, their alliances and their names, while in a series of referendums and in the 1965 Presidential Election, the electorate has overwhelmingly approved de Gaulle's policy of appealing directly to the voters and ignoring the politicians. This policy has inspired the opposition parties to more determined efforts to bridge their differences and present a common front in an effort to unseat him. These had a certain success in the tactical alliances between the FGDS and the PCF in 1965 and 1967. By March 1968 the partners were actively formulating a common electoral platform which seemed to threaten the whole structure of dogmatic anti-communism on which the Gaullist UNR had always relied. But when the crisis of the May Events came, the mutual fears, suspicions and hostilities on the left once again proved too strong for the tenuous bonds of unity and de Gaulle was able to triumph in the June elections by whipping up fears of 'a Communist takeover'.

13 · The main French political groupings

a) **The Gaullists** (Gretton)

A glance at the names that have been given to the various Gaullist movements is also instructive. The first was the short-lived Union Gaulliste of 1946. Following de Gaulle's Strasbourg speech in the spring of 1947 the Rassemblement du Peuple Français (Gathering of the French People) was then formed; although never officially dissolved, it ceased to be active after just over five years. After de Gaulle's return to power in 1958, the Union pour la Nouvelle République was founded on 1 October of that year; at the Lille conference in November 1967 it changed its name to Union des Démocrates pour la Cinquième République and, having fought the 1968 election under the banner of the Union pour la Défense de la République, it has now become Union de Démocrates pour la République. Although each of these organisations has taken part in the normal electoral process, they have without exception sought to distinguish themselves from political parties in the ordinary sense of the term, in particular by studiously avoiding the word 'party' in their names.

The reasons for this reveal a great deal about the nature of Gaullism. For Gaullists to describe themselves as a political party like any other would have meant accepting the traditional conception of representative democracy whereby each party represents a particular section (or interest group) of the population and all have equal right to exist. Now this is precisely what Gaullists do not accept; for them the only true Frenchmen are those who are prepared to be united (Union) or gathered together (Rassemblement) behind General de Gaulle. This has the inevitable corollary that all those who are not Gaullists are not true Frenchmen and are to be cast into outer darkness. Whence the extraordinary animosity of Gaullists towards non-Gaullists; political adversaries are not considered simply as opponents, but as veritable enemies, not to say traitors, to be feared and hated.

b) The Federation (Fédération de la Gauche Démocrate et Socialiste)
(Seale and McConville)

In December 1965 François Mitterand, a Socialist lawyer and politician who had started his career during the Fourth Republic, reaching the rank of junior minister, joined forces with the PCF in the Presidential Election, standing as the candidate of the whole Left. This marriage of convenience between the old rivals of the Left, Communism and Social Democracy, was extremely successful. Mitterand was able to attract enough votes to force De Gaulle into a second round to decide between them. This success made it possible for him to pursue the objective of forging a permanent alliance between the many different factions into which the non-Communist Left was divided. The main components of the Federation were: The Radicals, the oldest political party in France, in steady decline since the great days of the Third Republic, but still numbering some of the most experienced and gifted notables of French politics; the Convention of Republican Institutions—a loose grouping of about 60 clubs and societies of unaffiliated left-wing activists; and Guy Mollet's SFIO (Section française de l'internationale ouvrière) which had been set up by Léon Blum in 1920 after the majority of the French Socialist party had joined the Communist International. In working towards the creation of a unified Federation of the Left Mitterand's main supporters were the energetic and progressive young men of the 'ginger groups' of the Convention, while the main obstacle in his path was the long-established party bureaucracy of the SFIO which obstinately dragged its feet.

c) The Communists
(Seale and McConville)

The overriding aim of the French Communist Party in the last three years has been to emerge from the political wilderness in which it has languished since 1947, and to become acceptable as a participant in government. In spite of its large working-class vote, the party knows that it cannot realistically hope to muster a governing majority on its own. Its road to power within the parliamentary system must lie therefore in an alliance with the non-Communist Left. Hence its rapprochement with Mitterand's Federation.

The French Communist Party has been much maligned. De Gaulle can win an election by scaring the electorate with the spectre of a Communist revolution, but the truth is that the Communist Party has not been a revolutionary movement since the Second World War. This is partly because it was from its birth in 1920 a mass party, not an avant-garde splinter group like other European

Communist Parties. At the Tours Congress of December 1920 four-fifths of the SFIO decided to join the Comintern, one-fifth only following Léon Blum. The Communist Party was thus the direct heir of pre-First World War French socialism, and had a broad base to build from. It did not have to create a new organisation from scratch. Faithful to Soviet requirements it was however a genuinely revolutionary party in the twenties and early thirties, backing Léon Blum's Popular Front government in 1936 only as a temporary tactic.

Thrown back into clandestinity by the Nazi-Soviet pact of August 1939, the PCF staged a triumphant and patriotic come-back in the Resistance when Russia entered the war in June 1941. This was its finest hour: its militants demonstrated in action their capacity for sacrifice and the effectiveness of their cell-like organisation. Their reward came at the Liberation, with 26 per cent of the vote in the October 1945 elections and four key ministries in General de Gaulle's government. But they were finally excluded from power a year and seven months later when Paul Ramadier dropped them from his government in May 1947, and they have not tasted power since. In that short spell twenty-one years ago, the PCF became part of the governing system and it has retained a profound nostalgia for it. This is not a revolutionary instinct. Moreover, the large Communist electorate, which gives the Party credit for the great social reforms of 1936 and 1945–6 is itself profoundly reformist, not revolutionary. The Party has, in fact, been made in the image of its members, who are firmly integrated in society, no longer its alienated underdogs.

Such was the PCF on the eve of the May crisis: longing for respectability; committed to an alliance with the Federation as the only path towards the power it longed for; supported by an industrial working class which in its immense majority wanted consumer goods not revolution. It should be added that the Party's leadership was no longer in its first youth, that none were men of outstanding political gifts, and—last but not least—that the Soviet Union, to which the Party has remained undeviatingly faithful throughout its career, has plumped firmly for peaceful co-existence. The last thing the Kremlin wants is a revolution in France which would deprive Russia of the considerable support it derives from General de Gaulle's foreign policy.

14 · The achievements of ten years of Gaullism

'The Times',
30 May 1968

First and foremost General de Gaulle abandoned the French Empire and led his legions home with flying colours. The great adventure in Africa ended not as a humiliation but as a great moral victory. It was, of course, a piece of legerdemain that the man who rode to power on a coup d'état designed to preserve French Algeria should so quickly transform himself into the great de-coloniser.

... The second achievement was a complete recasting of relations between Europe and America. France, at least, and to a great extent Europe as a whole, are no longer American clients, and this is all to the good.

... His third achievement, until the beginning of this month, was seen to consist in establishing social peace, economic progress, secure political institutions, and an atmosphere of stability and peace. Indeed, in a whole series of press conferences, messages to the National Assembly and televised pronouncements, he claimed repeatedly that the choice was between himself and chaos.

15 · 'When France is Bored. . . .'

'Le Monde' (editorial), 15 March 1968

What characterises our public life at present is boredom. The French are bored. They are not taking part either directly or indirectly in the great convulsions which are shaking the world. . . . Nothing of all that touches us directly: anyway the television repeats at least three times an evening that France is at peace for the first time for over thirty years and that it is neither involved nor concerned with any other part of the world.

Youth is bored. The students are demonstrating and are active, are fighting in Spain, in Italy, in Belgium, in Algeria, in Japan, in America, in Egypt, in Germany, and even in Poland. They have the impression that they have battles to win, protests to make, at least a sentiment of the absurd to oppose to the general absurdity. French students are worried about whether the girls at Nanterre can have free access to the bedrooms of the boys, which is really rather a limited conception of the rights of man. . . . As for the young workers, they look for work and don't find it. The backslapping, the preaching and the exclamations of politicians of all parties appear to all these young people at best rather comic and at worst completely pointless, almost always incomprehensible.

General de Gaulle is bored. He had sworn that he would not inaugurate any more chrysanthemums and he is still going, benignly official, from the Salon de l'Agriculture to the Lyons Fair. What else has he got to do? Sometimes he tries, not very successfully, to dramatise daily life by exaggerating loudly the external dangers and the internal perils. Under his breath, he sighs about the flabbiness of his compatriots who nevertheless once more entrusted him with all their affairs. And of course the television never misses a chance to remind us that the Government is stable for the first time for a century.

Only a few hundred thousand Frenchmen are not bored: the out-of-work, the young men without jobs, the small peasants crushed by progress, victims of a necessary economic concentration and of competition getting fiercer and fiercer, old men more or less abandoned by everybody. These are so absorbed in their troubles that they have no time to be bored, nor have they the heart to demonstrate and agitate. Everyone else is bored with them. And so nothing disturbs the calm.

Crisis

5 · The Student Insurrection (1 – 13 May)

Chronology of the Crisis

Wednesday 1 May

More than 50,000 people march through Paris from the Place de la République to the Bastille. Such a May Day demonstration has not been seen since the Algerian War was at its height, in 1960.

Thursday 2 May

A right-wing student accuses Daniel Cohn-Bendit, one of the principal leaders of the extreme left-wing students of Nanterre, of having threatened him and having had him beaten up. The Civil Court of Paris opens a judicial enquiry against Cohn-Bendit. Nanterre closed. Pompidou leaves for Iran.

Friday 3 May

The extreme right-wing movement Occident starts fires in some parts of the University after announcing its intention to 'clean up the Sorbonne'.

The Nanterre students meet at the Sorbonne. The Rector requests the police to intervene against the students meeting under the chairmanship of Cohn-Bendit in the courtyard of the faculty. At 4 pm 527 students are arrested. The UNEF calls upon all left-wing organisations to protest against these measures and calls a strike. The newspaper of the PCF, L'Humanité, defines the students as 'drawing-room revolutionaries'.

One hour later the students organise a demonstration through the streets of Paris. The police intervene, indiscriminately clubbing students and passers-by. The clashes continue for more than five hours. The polie use tear-gas grenades. Over 100 wounded.

Saturday 4 May

UNEF announces a protest demonstration in the Quartier Latin for Monday, 6 May.

Sunday 5 May

Four of the arrested students are tried under emergency procedure and condemned to heavy prison sentences. The police interrogate the leaders of the students, Cohn-Bendit and Sauvageot, for 24 hours. The Prefect of Police, Grimaud, forbids all demonstrations, and the police move into the Quartier Latin in force.

Monday 6 May

From early morning thousands of students respond to the appeal of the UNEF and begin to flow into the Quartier Latin to take part in the demonstration called for 6.30 pm. In the afternoon about 3 pm, the police angered by the taunts of the students ('Free our comrades', 'The Sorbonne to the students', 'We are a splinter group', 'A handful of hotheads') charge them violently. The students then erect barricades in the Boulevard St Germain. For two hours the police attempt to destroy these. The battle continues until late at night, despite the fact that the UNEF asks the demonstrators to disperse:

there are 422 arrests and 600 students wounded and 345 police. SNE Sup. calls a strike. De Gaulle declares: 'We cannot tolerate violence in the streets!'. Georges Séguy, Secretary General of the CGT, declares: 'There is a tradition which forces us not to tolerate the provocatory elements who denigrate the working class by accusing it of becoming bourgeois and make the impudent claim of being able to teach us what revolution is and to direct our struggle'. The other two trades unions, the CFDT and the FO, express their disapproval of 'student violence'. 100 MJR supporters join the students.

Tuesday 7 May

A procession of 30–40,000 students marches across Paris. The Internationale is sung over the Eternal Flame of the Unknown Soldier. The students demand: (i) the suspension of legal proceedings; (ii) the withdrawal of police from the Quartier Latin; (iii) the re-opening of the faculties.

In the Quartier Latin the students clash with the police who throw tear-gas grenades (also into the Café Select). The battle goes on until 3.30 am.

Wednesday 8 May

The National Assembly meets in extraordinary session. The Education Minister, Peyrefitte, declares: 'When all the disorders are over, the faculties will be re-opened'. The CGT and the CFDT declare their solidarity with the students during a meeting at the Faculty of Sciences, but the representative of the CGT is whistled and called an opportunist. 20,000 students and teachers demonstrate, but thanks to their own marshals there is no clash with the police. At the National Assembly Mitterrand accuses the Government: 'You have treated the students as objects and you have obtained violence. This is the consequence of your policy!'

Thursday 9 May

Students arriving at the Sorbonne find it closed, and gather in the Quartier Latin. The UNEF contacts the trades unions to organise a common demonstration. The SNE Sup. and the UNEF declare that the strike goes on. Open meeting of the JCR. Sauvageot: 'We shall continue the strike until our three points are conceded' 'Calm has not returned' says Peyrefitte. Rector Roche: 'The disciplinary committee of the university will not postpone its meeting'.

Friday 10 May

The Faculty at Nanterre is re-opened (and promptly occupied by the students), but the Sorbonne remains closed. A demonstration is called for 6.30 pm, at Place Denfert-Rocherau by the UNEF and the SNE Sup. After a long detour 30,000 move towards the Quartier Latin, despite appeals to disperse by members of the UEC.

The demonstrators begin to erect barricades. Until 1 am Cohn-Bendit, Sauvageot and Geismar attempt to negotiate on the three points with the Minister, using Roche as an intermediary. Denouncing 'adventurism', the FER contingent leaves the scene en bloc. The barricades already number about sixty. At 2.15 am the police receive the order to destroy them. The demonstrators resist on the barricades of Rue Gay Lussac until 6 am. As well as tear-gas the police use poison-gas, paralysing-gas and incendiary bombs. Students reply with cobbles and Molotov cocktails. Many people not involved in the demonstrations are arrested and beaten up. The wounded in hospitals number 367 (including 251 Police), 468 people are arrested and 188 cars are destroyed.

Saturday 11 May

The Prime Minister, Pompidou, returns to Paris from Iran and accepts the UNEF demands. The CGT, the CFDT and then the FO accept the UNEF proposal to declare a general strike for 12 May. Clashes in the Quartier Latin. Student occupation of faculties at Nanterre, Strasbourg, Bordeaux, Rennes and the Sorbonne annexe in the Rue Censier. Three Nobel prize-winners, A. Kastler, J. Monod and J. Lwolf, declare that they will be in the Quartier Latin with the demonstrators.

Sunday 12 May

The parties of the Left begin to make attempts to take over the direction of the student movements. After eight hours of discussions the trade unions of the students and the workers organise a common demonstration for Monday 13 May from Place de la République to Place Denfert-Rocherau at 3.30 pm.

Monday 13 May

General Strike. About 700,000 people demonstrate in Paris. Protest marches in many big towns. The police do not intervene. The CGT attempts to prevent contact between students and workers. At Place Denfert-Rocherau, the terminal point, it gives the order to disperse. But many workers continue as far as the Champ de Mars where, on the initiative of the Mouvement du 22 mars, a dialogue begins between the students and the workers. Later the Sorbonne is occupied after being evacuated by the police.

16 · How it started: where the authorities went wrong

'Le Monde' (Sélection hebdomadaire)
8 May 1968

On the 6 May Paris was the scene of the biggest and most serious student demonstration for decades. Even during the Algerian war the student protest movement did not achieve such proportions nor last so long.

The rector of the Sorbonne, M. Roche, and the Minister of Education had calculated that at a time when students are feverishly revising for their examinations, very few of them would bother to turn out in support of the 'trouble-makers' of Nanterre, arrested on the orders of M. Peyrefitte. Both of them were quite wrong.

At the very moment when the Minister was calmly announcing on the radio and TV that these demonstrations had nothing in common with those that had been taking place in Berlin or Warsaw, over a thousand students were already on the streets.

Here, in the same way as abroad, a new phenomenon has been observed: a wave of solidarity among the students in support of their comrades in trouble and a readiness to go out and do 'battle' with the police. Linking arms the students stood their ground with extreme violence.

Such a wave of anger would not have occurred if the authorities had shown greater coolness of judgement on Friday 3 May. In order to justify the decisions he took and, as he stated himself, to

'back up the rector', the Minister has given an extremely misleading picture of recent events. In order to explain what he continues to call the suspension of classes at the Sorbonne (when in fact the faculty is closed), he has made out that there had already been blood-shed there. To our knowledge there was nothing of the sort. Moreover, all the witnesses of the demonstration of 3 May which took place in the courtyard of the Sorbonne are unanimous in saying that it passed off without any incidents.

This famous courtyard had seen more violent meetings by far in the past, it being the traditional rallying-place of the students. The only 'escalation', and it is an alarming one, is that the students have now begun to provide themselves in greater numbers with helmets and weapons. This is true of students of both left and right. It is on this point that the authorities most need to act. It is quite justifiable to bring those armed with clubs and axes before the courts without delay. But, here too, a warning should have been issued before action was taken.

By resorting at once to extreme measures, M. Peyrefitte, the former diplomatist, has got himself into a blind alley.

What should be done now that all the official prohibitions have been scorned so openly? The students will go on demonstrating despite the ban; many teachers and lecturers in Paris and in the provinces have gone on strike despite the Minister's warning about such action being illegal without due notice being given. Calm will not now be restored until the authorities set about creating a 'de-escalation'.

17 · Why the students hated the police

This article gives an insight into police behaviour and the instinctive reliance of Gaullism on violent repression.

The 'Guardian', 29 May 1968

The fact that we all, journalists particularly, tend to accept the terms and the phraseology of the Establishment often makes it difficult for readers to understand what has really happened. When we report, for example, that the 'arrest' of students who had demonstrated in the grounds of the Sorbonne led, three weeks ago, to a spontaneous and violent demonstration by ten times the number of students originally involved, this can puzzle the reader because of the apparently exaggerated reaction of the students. But not when you know that to 'arrest' often means to be flung headlong into a police van and be immediately assaulted within hearing of any bystanders.

Foreign journalists have almost always gone along with the official-ly underlined chief characteristic of Gaullism; its preoccupation with grandeur; its cosmic view of history. But in strict reality—the reality of living within the area where it directly operates—the regime has been consistently identified with conspiracy and violence. No one who lived through the last years of the Algerian war, who knows even a little about the Ben Barka affair, or who witnessed the automatic resort to violence, even in a 'cultural' affair like that of the Cinémathèque, can doubt that the regime has favoured, and believed, misguidedly as it is now clear, in the efficacy of violence.

During these past three weeks, the riot police were not just called out to contain demonstrators; they were let loose on the population. Many injuries came, not of direct, headlong clashes with the police, but when the police put the demonstrators to flight with tear gas grenades and then picked off those who fell behind. It was commonplace to see three or four police bludgeoning one cornered demonstrator. They assaulted those who tried to help the wounded, fired grenades into cafés and apartments from Saint Michel to Montparnasse and, as the days passed, it became commonplace for them to break into apartments and beat up the inhabitants. Doctors repeatedly reported that the police refused to let the ambulances get to the wounded, and last Thursday night the nurses and doctors at the Sorbonne told me that the police had fired a grenade into the infirmary. At night, long after the demonstrations were over, riot police continued to roam the streets looking for victims.

18 · Heart of the revolt: the courtyard of the Sorbonne

The 'New Statesman', 24 May 1968

In the courtyard of the Faculty of Letters, the heart and brain of the movement, a thousand flowers not only bloom but load the spring air with intellectual incense. Young socialists, Marxist Christians, Maoists, anti-CP Marxist-Leninists, Guevarists, Fidelistos, Breton nationalists, Young Workers, Portuguese democrats, Basques and Spaniards, young people from Germany and France and

Britain, shout their wares and debate their principles. On the walls, posters—some of great beauty, hand-painted in the École des Beaux Arts—proclaim a score of different creeds. In the over-flowing lecture halls and corri-dors, every conceivable topic is examined: forms of revolutionary action, birth control, the nature of the state, how to fight the police, workers' control, free love, the role of parents, the uses of exams, Vietnam, marriage and divorce, the nature of the univer-sity. There is, appropriately, a pentacostal mood, in which those speaking different tongues evoke a common understanding. Work-ers come there to argue and listen, and so do old men and house-wives, and foreigners and Depu-ties and writers and journalists.

The debating groups spill out into nearby streets and crowd the vast Odéon Theatre. De Gaulle, falling back, in his rage, on the vernacular of a young subaltern, has called it a 'dog's breakfast'. Perhaps it is, in a sense: France has brought up its Gaullist vomit and now feels better.

But the disparate debate is underpinned by a powerful thread of logic, which has transformed the French movement from a student revolt into a political event. Most of us, all along, have missed the real significance of the students' demands, partly through blindness, partly because they were not clearly articulated. Yes, we say, we agree you have a right to reforms in your universities, to greater control in their direc-tion and more say in their curri-

cula; but what has this to do with more general political action? Why don't you stick to your own business? It has taken the French to get the argument across, and I doubt if even they could have done it without the leadership of Cohn-Bendit. This jovial young Robe-spierre, with his flaming red hair and piercing blue eyes, has the true revolutionary's gift of combining a philosophy which can be rea-soned, slogans which can be shouted and a mad-dog taste for taking positions by frontal assault. When he speaks, men listen; where he leads, they follow. He makes the impossible become possible simply by doing it. It wouldn't surprise me if he beats the ban on his return to France.

19 · The stirrers-up of strife

'Le Nouvel Observateur', 19 June 1968

Who are the 'splinter-groups' which have been dissolved for the moment but who during a whole month made the regime tremble?

At first, at the time of Nanterre, 'they' were not all in agreement, far from it. But they did agree on one position which seemed funda-mental to them: to throw off the shackles of all the traditional political movements. To gamble on lack of organisation. The Mouvement du 22 mars launched a notion absent from the voca-bulary of all previous movements, precisely: spontaneism. And if it is really a 'movement', it is some-thing like a movement which pro-vokes the movement which creates the movement etc. It is the spark

at the heart of the student move-ment which is itself a spark.

From the beginning the UJCM-L (pro-Chinese) revealed their dif-ference from the others in a leaflet. They said that the move-ment was '100 per cent bourgeois'. There were protests from the floor of the meeting, and the 'Chinese', having first walked out, returned later with clenched fists and singing the Internationale: one of their leaders declared: 'The UJCM-L of Paris has decided to leave Nanterre and not to give any help in guarding the faculty'. As far as the UJCM-L is con-cerned what is important is not happening in the Sorbonne, but in the factories and at the factory gates. The students are only petit-bourgeois elements, it is the working class which is the standard-bearer in the struggle.

At first, every evening, on the

steps in front of the chapel, with their Mao badge in their button-holes, the UJCM-L held a public meeting. It was always extremely vehement. But soon, their activity inside the Sorbonne was no longer limited to the sale of their papers, at their table: *Serve the People*, plus the daily paper which they brought out themselves during the events, *The Cause of the People*; with, naturally, the *Thoughts of Mao* in innumerable copies. The great majority of the 'Chinese' spent their time at the factories. If they denounced the 'treachery' of the leaders of the working-class, they encouraged the workers to carry the struggle on inside the CGT. They would have nothing to do with the CFDT. They denounced the meeting at Charléty.

Yet on that day, there were 40,000 people in the stands and

in the arena. The Anarchists distinguished themselves at the start by a dazzling Indian war-dance all round the race track, with their black flags flowing in the wind. 'And to think that it took de Gaulle to bring that lot back!' cursed a witness, possibly a policeman. But whether they were whistled or acclaimed, the Anarchists did not care.

Split up into groups, and tendencies, they had only just regained some unity. There was the Anarchist Federation, which belongs particularly to the Organisation of Revolutionary Anarchists, and which brings out the paper *The World of Freedom*; more specialised groups in certain forms of struggle, particularly 'Noir et Rouge'; there were anarchists with Communist tendencies such as the JAC, the schoolboy organisation with about 60 militants in Paris and its suburbs; the Anarcho-Syndicalists, organised in a confederation, whilst the Federation organised itself on a communal basis.

At all the demonstrations, all the barricades, there they are. One cannot really speak of an anarchist political activity: but only of an undeniable anarchist presence:

'We have been on all the demos and all the same we don't like walking! Moreover, the paper policemen's hats worn by the CGT, the whole carnival atmosphere really turned us on.... However, when there is a scrap going on we don't take to our heels.'

They don't deny that they have their own barricades. Theirs were the five barricades at the Rue de la Contrescarpe: 'those that held out longest'. The events of May hinged on the question of authority and of its most obvious representative, political power: so they were naturally favourable

to the student movement:

'But mind! In the view of the Anarchist Federation, there is no question of reviving Marxism... Marxism is the opium of the average proletarian!'

But they certainly do believe in 'the great day':

'The revolution will come!... only there won't be a socialist state: there will just be socialism.'

At the Sorbonne, on the whole, they were regarded as being rather decent. How can I describe what I found out about them? Perhaps it was the feeling of a certain anarchist 'warm-hearted-ness'.

Faced with the FER one gets rather the opposite feeling.

They are Lambertist Trotskyites; they are directly linked to the International Communist Organisation, which broke away from the Fourth International, in 1952 after the disagreement between Lambert and Frank. In order to make capital from the crisis of Stalinism, Frank was advocating 'working from within' the mass organisations—whilst the Lambert fraction was against this.

Since then, other political differences have been evident. In particular, in connection with the 'colonial revolution'. The Lambertist position about Cuba is that Cuba is a bourgeois state which has been set up by petit-bourgeois adventurists called Castro and Guevara. On the NLF, this is merely an emanation of the petite-bourgeoisie of Vietnam. They refused to sign the appeal for an end to the war in Vietnam.

On the first night of the barricades the FER was cut off from the movement as a whole. On Friday 10th May, at half past eleven in the evening, they left the student union and set off in a body, about a thousand of them, along the Boulevard St Michel. They stopped halfway down how-

ever: 'Comrades, we warn you that you are going to a massacre, this is sheer adventurism!' Nobody followed them: they were reproached for not following the movement.

Ever since that night, every time a member of the FER tries to speak through the microphone at the Sorbonne, a voice or several voices shout a question, always the same one:

'And on the night of the barricades, where were you?'

The slogans of the FER are: '500,000 workers in the streets'; '1,000,000 workers before the Elysée'; '3,500 young people at the Sorbonne in June'; and finally, and always, 'United Front':

'It is just verbal escalation! One slogan is fine, it has a certain revolutionary virtue, but only if it is taken up by the masses! But they shout slogans like releasing balloons; it only comes down three months later; and then they accuse the 'treacherous leaders' of not having followed them... It is too easy!', say many students, who are not being convinced by them.

At the demos, the FER marches in closed ranks, compact, singing at the tops of their voices; with a marshalling system which is first class. But at the Sorbonne, they were hard to find. On staircase C, on the second floor; they had not been seen in the courtyard since the early days. All the same, they are to be found there in the evenings, all mobilised to sell their paper:

'For the creation of a central strike committee, for an unlimited strike, buy *Révoltes*!'

Otherwise, 'they only go to other people's meetings in order to muck things up'. In fact, the evening that Daniel Cohn-Bendit got back from Germany, they tried to steal the show from him; but the meeting threw them out.

Another evening, the whole great lecture hall stood for five minutes shouting 'FER fascists! FER fascists!'

At first, one is surprised, one does not understand, one wonders why they are regarded as being so insufferable. . . . It is a question of political attitudes, but also of style and tone. Their martial air, their strong-arm methods, the way they resort to insult and threat, the deliberately 'working class' banter and chaff, is not very popular in the Latin Quarter:

' "Putting the frighteners on" is all right for the twerps from Occident. But not for people on the Left.'

Finally, the JCR, their main 'rival' in the old battle between the Trotskyites. But mostly they are expellees from the UEC when, in 1965, they refused to back the candidature of François Mitterrand for the presidency. They have their own paper: *The Youth Vanguard*. Like the Anarchists, the JCR are free and easy. They are decent people, they smile, they are 'civilised': but a JCR meeting is all the same a working session. Real work, documented, without idle chatter—but also, an intellectual firework display. Moreover it is an *open* meeting: everybody can take part, say that he doesn't agree, argue. Their respect for different points of view is a sacred principle to them.

They were the only ones, together with the Mouvement du 22 mars, to be able to fill the big amphitheatre.

They are certainly revolutionaries. They have always said they are. They have always declared that the tide of revolution which is flowing today in the world is posing the problem of 'world socialism'. But they have never acted like a gang or a secret organisation trying to plot the downfall of capitalism from the shadows! Yet they too have been arrested. France is, after all, a capitalist country and to speak of socialism there is quite enough to make it shudder. There are certain ideas which are more frightening than rifles.

20 · The techniques of demonstrations

'Le Nouvel Observateur',
15 May 1968

It would be 'reassuring' if all these young people had been taken in hand by professional agitators, if they had been nothing but raw material. It would be very comforting to think that their revolt was guided by elements parachuted in, by specialists in urban guerilla warfare, specialists in subversion.

However, it is enough to see how things actually happened to discard this hypothesis. A specialist in urban guerilla warfare would never have decided to construct barricades in the Rue Gay Lussac, which is too wide and made it easier for the police to shower the defenders with grenades. He would not have constructed barricades so close to each other, either, or so hermetically sealed as to imprison their defenders.

But it is not difficult for the students to understand a few simple rules and, moreover, everyone was wonderfully familiar with the district where the fighting took place. This was not the case with the CRS (riot police) who were from Marseille, Lille or Dijon. The student marshalling organisation is extremely impressive. Each organisation possesses its own. During the last few days those of UNEF and of the JCR have played a capital role. During the course of the great demonstrations of the other week, a swarm of scouts and despatch riders on bicycles or mopeds kept on weaving back and forth between the leading ranks of the demonstration and the police cordons. On the other hand, students who had taken up positions right along the route in private houses or in cafés would inform the organisers of the student marshals by telephone of what was happening: thus from minute to minute the latter were kept abreast of what was happening on the police side as well as on the student side, and knew where the CRS buses were heading.

At the same time, another network, just as perfect and discreet, was at work. It was that of the police. At regular intervals the demonstrators were counted. It was in this way that on Friday evening about 8 o'clock, police realised that about 2,000 demonstrators had disappeared in a very brief space of time. Even reckoning that some of them had gone to bed, it was puzzling to know where the others had gone. The CRS realised where when they found various projectiles landing on their heads, flung from the nearby roofs.

When the two groups were facing each other on open ground, which was practically always the case up till the night of the 10th May, the rear of the procession began to pull up the cobblestones from the streets. Here again, it was a simple and new technique. The tools that they needed were found on the spot: most often part of the metal grid protecting the tree roots. When the cobblestones had been prised loose, a human chain was formed to pass them forward to the head of the demonstration. The use of cobblestones is a novelty and showed itself extremely effective: at first because it can cause quite serious injuries, and secondly because the police are hard-put to defend themselves from it when they have neither the right, nor with their backs to their own coaches, the chance to retreat.

The response of the police is also quite simple. They throw by hand the first shower of tear-gas grenades, to form a screen right across the street. The second shower is sent about ten yards further from they by using grenade throwers, in order to separate the head of the demonstration from the mass. During this time, the students have been able to throw several salvos of cobblestones.

It is generally at this moment that the first charge starts. The task of attacking along the pavements is reserved to special sections of the police whose job is to break the demonstrators' front line. It is then that usually the worst and blindest clobberings with police truncheons take place.

21 · The Battle of the Rue Gay Lussac

The 'New Statesman', 17 May 1968

The decision to stage what was virtually a military occupation of the Sorbonne, at the climax of the academic year, had the predictable effect. It turned the entire student body, overnight, into supporters of the Cohn-Bendit strategy, made the resources and organisation of the official students' union available for direct action, and swung the great majority of parents and university staff behind the protest movement. The imprisonment of four students added an element of personal victimisation and supplied a slogan behind which all could unite: *Libérez nos camérades!* On Friday night, an inspired fever gripped 30,000 students gathered round the occupied buildings of the Sorbonne. Boys and girls, ripping out the paving stones with their bare hands, performed prodigious physical feats in setting up their barricades, in a desperate attempt to protect their bodies as well as their liberties. If the police were to clear the streets at all—and this was bound to lead to some bloodshed—they should have been ordered to advance immediately the students began their defensive preparations. Instead several hours were spent on futile negotiations, while the barricades mounted higher. Then, at 2.15 in the morning, ministers gave the insensate command to attack. The security forces, ignoring the pitiful efforts of the students to stage a purely passive resistance, fell on them as though they had been an armed enemy.

The details of that terrible night are still coming in. The police used hundreds of gas-bombs and grenades. Official claims that only 'conventional' tear-gas was used are not believed. Even earlier in the week the police, pursuing wounded students who had taken refuge in a bookshop in the Rue Saint Séverin, hurled grenades through the door; five assistants there were badly hurt and the doctor who treated them consider that the damage to their eyes was not consistent with the use of ordinary tear-gas. After a meeting of doctors held last Saturday at a hospital in the Rue Saint Antoine, Dr François Kahn announced that gas containing a combination of smoke, tear-gas and incendiary elements had been used earlier that day, and produced a plastic grenade, found on the scene of battle, filled with white phosphorous and four other agents. The condition of some of the injured was consistent with the use of an American-type nerve gas. One student had his hand blown off by an explosive grenade.

Most of the injuries were the result of the vicious and indiscriminate use of heavy truncheons, chiefly on the head and legs (several students had fractured legs). Anyone who demonstrates in Paris must expect to get his (or her) head broken. But on this occasion the police exhibited a persistent brutality for which there is no parallel in recent decades. They made no distinctions of sex or age, battering unconscious both young girls and middle-aged lecturers. Householders in the quarter were treated like an occupied population. The retreating students implored those living in the streets to pour water through the windows, to disperse the gas. Many did. The police battered on their doors, called out *Fermez les fenêtres!*' and, in at least one case, hurled a grenade through the window of a man who did not immediately comply. Long after the student resistance was broken, and the barricades stormed, the police hunted down fugitives, breaking into private houses and cafés, and demanding that students—including those already injured—should be surrendered to them. The householders had no particular cause to love the students, for many of them had already suffered damage to their property; but they tried to protect them because they knew that, once in the police vans, they would be systematically beaten—as, indeed, happened in many, many cases. Captured students knelt, huddled in groups in the middle of the streets, their hands protecting their heads against the *matraques*. People who had nothing to do with the demonstration were assaulted, men and women alike. Students were asked to show their hands: those with dirt on them were assumed to have helped to build the barricades, and treated accordingly.

Most shocking of all were assaults on those already injured. Professor Daniel Lacombe informed *Le Monde* that the police broke into a Red Cross post in the Institut Henri Poincaré, and beat him up; Pasteur Roger Parmentier likewise testifies that the injured were dragged from their stretchers and that the police beat both the sick and those trying to look after them. Long into Saturday, students were still hiding in cellars and houses, afraid to come out. No doubt the police were scared—and with reason—and angered by their own heavy casualties. But their behaviour has left Paris sickened and embittered.

22 · Trotskyite students' defiance

Statement made before the disciplinary committee of the University of Paris, Monday 6 May at 11.00

Gentlemen,
I challenge you,
I challenge the disciplinary council,
I challenge your tribunal.

Gentlemen, I am not challenging you as professors, my tutors, whose job it is to impart to a student such as myself the knowledge and culture which I need for the profession I intend to take up.

I challenge you, because you are gathered here today, acting on the orders of a Government and State, which, by means of selection and massive elimination has decided to turn out of the University two-thirds of the students whom one of your colleagues, the Rector Capelle, previously described as waste products.

I challenge you, because I find before me today not my professors, but men who have agreed to carry out the work of the CRS and to endorse the unprecedented decision to close the Sorbonne.

I challenge you, because whatever your verdict may be, I wish to remain proud of my name and the sacrifices that my father, a metal worker, made in order that I might continue my studies. Like all workers, my father has to bear the burden of the governmental measures decided by the 5th Plan, which include the police-style educational reforms that you accept.

In challenging you, Gentlemen, I realise that I am defending not only the right to study and freedom in the university, but also your positions as professors, your mission as teachers, your own dignity. At the moment, Gentlemen my judges, I shall not reply to any of your questions.

Michael Pourny
UNEF Militant
Member of the national bureau of the FER

23 · Appeal to all Parisians

One of the students' attempts to mobilise public opinion in their support

Appeal to all Parisians

There may be 'splinter groups who want action at any price'
But there are also
    'Millions who want inaction at any price'
who smugly accept from the depths of their armchairs whatever
is put out by the press or the ORTF or merely the gossip of their
neighbours.
        Parisians
We do not ask you to act
We do not ask you to defend us
We just say that it is
        Your duty
To be there, in the streets or even at your windows
To be there, passive if you do not want to act, but
To be there,
        present
        for
    the force of eyes watching
        is a
    force of justice
        The truncheons
will not dare get busy if you are watching them
with
        millions of eyes.

24 · Voice of the walls

Perhaps the most spontaneous and authentic expression of the student viewpoint during the May Events was to be found in the slogans painted and chalked by the thousands everywhere in Paris. We can only give a small selection, but even these few demonstrate the amazing diversity of imagination that was inspired by the Events.

Let's open the gates of nurseries, universities, and other prisons.
Thanks to teachers and exams competitiveness starts at six.
Kiss your love without leaving your gun.
Be a realist, demand the impossible.
Those who make a revolution by halves, dig their own graves.
A Philistine's tears are the nectar of the gods.
I take my desires for reality, because I believe in the reality of my
    desires.[1]
Society is a carnivorous flower.
When the General Assembly becomes a bourgeois theatre,
    bourgeois theatres must become the General Assembly.
Rape your alma mater.
We won't ask, we won't demand, we will take and occupy.
There are no revolutionary thoughts, only revolutionary actions.

[1] The PCF continually criticised the 'Leftists' for 'taking their desires for reality.'

When the last capitalist is hanged with the guts of the last
   reformist, humanity will be happy.
Run forward comrade, the old world is behind you.
Ten days of happiness already.
Freedom is the consciousness of our desires.
The general will against the will of the General.
When the unpredictable has happened, the seemingly impossible
   is at hand.
It is forbidden to forbid.
To live means to re-invent life.
Et alors Fouchet, ça gaze? (note the pun between ça gaze =
   everything O.K. and ça gaze = it gasses.)
Imagine new forms of sexual perversion.
Be homosexuals. (To which somebody else had added 'Women and
   children first')
To act is to become aware.
Who creates, and for whom?
Rêve + évolution = révolution. (Rêve = dream)
Let's make an omelette; the eggs we shall break are only potential
   chickens.
Let those who want to make revolution take up arms; let those
   who want to demonstrate take up the cobbles.
Neither slaves nor robots; neither work nor leisure.
There are no master thinkers, it is thought which is the master.
When law and order suppress free speech, cobblestones replace it.
Humanity is not a condition to be borne, it is a dignity to be
   conquered.
Whoever is not me, is an agent of the repression which is being
   carried out against me.
An intellectual is judged not by what he thinks but by the relation-
   ship between what he thinks and what he does.
After the universities and the factories let us occupy public opinion.
Not to repress what oppresses us is the best repression against
   those who repress us.
Write your ideas on walls; it makes them dirty but it's good for you.

25 · 'Our commune of 10th May': Cohn-Bendit

This is the ending of a long article on Cohn-Bendit which was the result of an interview with him immediately after the first wave of student riots in the Latin Quarter. In the article Cohn-Bendit first describes the strategy and tactics of the struggle in the streets and then goes on to deal with the difficult situation arising from the attempts to cooperate with the trades unions and the Communist Party. (In referring to the students' 'Commune', Cohn-Bendit is deliberately evoking a comparison with the 'Paris Commune' [insurrection] of 1871).

**'Le Nouvel Observateur',
15 May 1968**

People are saying to us now: you've got some results it's true, but it's cost you hundreds of wounded and perhaps—we'll find out in the end—several deaths. Wasn't it too high a price to pay for your success? I reply: it wasn't us who were in a position to decide whether there would be wounded and dead or not. It is those in power. We have been surprised ourselves by the unbelievable imbecility of the authorities. We had not foreseen any trial of strength in spring.

According to our analysis, everything should have started when the students came back next autumn. At that time there would have been an objective situation—a shortage of premises and teachers, disorganisation and inefficiency in the teaching—which would push the students towards violence because they would have been able to realise by then that the strikes and peaceful demonstrations of the previous year had served no purpose. The crisis took place sooner because those in power unleashed it themselves. And once the escalation had begun we were obliged to follow them.

During Friday 3 May, when the police invaded the Sorbonne, nobody in the student movement wanted it to happen. But what happened was that the students of their own accord, without any orders, turned around and fought back. From that moment on it was impossible to go into reverse without seeming to betray those who instead of fleeing had accepted the clash. The violence that occurred was not due to those in charge of the movement deciding that there should be violence; it was the students who spontaneously chose to resist. After that it was inconceivable that the leaders should say: 'Hey, boys, we're packing it in, it's getting too dangerous.' Those in power would have said: 'See, even those in charge of the extreme Left are backing away from the groups of hotheads who acted on 3 May'.

Subsequently, of course, there have been even more wounded, there have been terrible scenes. But how can we be made responsible for this? It is the system which is violent, it is society which is violent. Yes, our resistance to the violence of the Government—because it was the Government after all which sent its policemen against us, with their batons and their grenades—caused many people to be wounded. Many young people have been wounded physically. But the young workers I was talking about just now, those who manned the barricade in the Rue le Goff, they had an interior wound which is perhaps more serious. Bourgeois hypocrisy consists of saying: it is better to perpetuate interior wounds, which are not seen, than to risk bloodshed. But I don't think so. In any case we weren't given the choice.

We never dreamed of issuing the order: 'Everyone into the street and fight!' Nobody would have followed us. We believe that a movement arises when an objective situation justifies it and causes it. We thought, as I said, that this objective situation would exist next autumn when the university students returned. The stupidity of the Government has created it in May. We had nothing to do with it.

In fact, what has happened in Paris, on a greater scale and more quickly, is what has been happening for months at Nanterre. Every time that we denounced something and that a trial of strength had begun, we realised that an ever-growing number of students were joining our campaign. Because they realised that what we were denouncing was true, and confirmed by the facts every time. Our programme, now that we have had an initial success, is quite simple: not to let the movement disintegrate, to continue to explain, to denounce, and to act.

26 · The Teachers in support

Extract from an article by Alain Touraine, Professor of Sociology at Nanterre.

**'Le Monde',
11 May 1968**

The students who are in revolt feel that they are imprisoned and repressed by the teaching system, by the university, by society itself. To talk to them about the 'objective' needs of society is the same thing as confining them within bounds which may be more modern than those which are traditional but are still more hurtful. It is no reply to the demands of the workers to tell them that the needs of economic growth require them to sacrifice their qualifications, their jobs or their homes. The transformations which are necessary have an entirely different sense according to whether the workers are aware or not of exercising some real control over the ends and the means of social change. The university situation is of the same kind.

The teachers who today recognise and defend the student movement can contribute to defuse a situation that repression is making more and more explosive. It is not a question of identifying themselves with a movement in which they are not the real actors, but no more is it a question of taking up a stance of protective neutrality. Tomorrow it will be necessary to discuss; but this cannot be done without first stating that those with whom you will sometimes agree and sometimes disagree must first be recognised and not crushed. The debate of tomorrow supposes the solidarity of today.

27 · The Gaullist attitude develops

a) **Communiqué issued by the Ministry of Education. (Excerpt) 7 May 1968**

... If some students should try to disrupt the examinations, they would be immediately be brought before the competent university authorities so that they could be expelled. In fact, the normal functioning of the examinations constitutes in this period of the year the main preoccupation of virtually all the teachers and students.

b) **Semi-official note released by the France-Presse Agency 10 May 1968 (about 10 a.m.)**

It is stated this morning in Government quarters that during the demonstrations last night in the Quartier Latin forces hostile to the return of peace in Vietnam took part, whilst negotiations on Vietnam between Americans and North Vietnamese are taking place in Paris.

The same quarters stress the difference between the mass of students and the hard core of 'activists' since the beginning of the incidents.

c) **Statement made by M. Georges Pompidou late on the Saturday night immediately on his return from his tour of Iran and Afghanistan. (Excerpt) 11 May 1968**

'As soon as I got back three hours ago, I convened a meeting of the Ministers concerned and after conferring with the President of the Republic, and with his agreement, I decided that the Sorbonne would be freely re-opened from Monday next, and that the courses should recommence at the discretion of the Rector and the Deans.

Measures will be taken ensuring that the candidates for the examinations should not suffer any delays in their work.

From Monday also, the court of appeal will be able in conformity with the law to pronounce on the requests for release presented by the students who have been sentenced.

These decisions are inspired by deep sympathy for the students and by confidence in their common sense. ...

I ask everybody, and particularly the leaders of the representative organisations of the students, to reject the provocations of certain professional agitators and to cooperate in a rapid and total return of peace. I am prepared to do my part towards such a return.

Let my appeal be heard by everybody'!

28 · The Communist attitude develops

a) **Statement of the UEC, 6 May 1968**

The leaders of the Leftists use the pretext of the failures of the Government and speculate on the discontent of the students in order to try to prevent the faculties from functioning and to prevent the mass of students from working and passing their exams. Thus, these false revolutionaries are objectively behaving as allies of the Gaullist Government and of its policy which is damaging students as a whole, and particularly those whose origins are not middle-class.

b) **Statement (excerpt) made by Georges Séguy of the CGT, 7 May 1968**

Solidarity between students, teachers, and working class is a familiar notion to all the militants of the CGT. It is a tradition which compels us rightly to have no patience with trouble-making and provocative elements who denigrate the working-class. The French working class has no need of petit-bourgeois leadership. It can find among its own class the experienced leaders and cadres that it needs.

c) **Declaration made by Waldeck Rochet, Secretary of the PCF 11 May 1968**

The French Communist Party condemns this fierce repression and expresses the indignant protests of the workers, the intellectuals, and the youth. It demands: the immediate and total ending of the repression; the withdrawal of the police forces from the Quartier Latin; an amnesty for the demonstrators who have been sentenced, and the immediate release of those in prison, and an end to further prosecution; the reopening of the faculties.

29 · A dissenting Gaullist

Excerpt from a speech made by the former Minister of Agriculture, M. Edgar Pisani during the debate on the riots in the Quartier Latin 9 May 1968

Before my son and his friends I sometimes have to remain silent, or to lie because I cannot always find a reply to the question that they ask me. A great deal has been said about a 'handful of agitators' who are supposed to be the only people responsible for these demonstrations. I warn you, Mr Minister, against the temptation only to be concerned with them and not to consider the problems of the others. The agitators and the mass of demonstrators are united by the same anguish. Your task is to ensure that the latter do not necessarily feel solidarity with the former.

In reply M. Peyrefitte said 'I can say no more than this: if order is re-established, everything is possible; if it is not, nothing is possible'.

30 · Mitterrand speaks for the Opposition

Excerpt from M. Mitterrand's speech in the same debate, 9 May 1968

You have constantly treated students as objects. You have said that you were seeking a dialogue, that you did not wish for violence: but in reality you have refused dialogue and you have obtained violence. That is the measure of your policy. A régime which has put an end to the joint management of student social welfare, which abolished grants to the main student organisation, which has allowed the sources of dialogue to dry up, cannot in any case be believed, when the crisis comes, by those to whom it speaks. If youth is not always right, society when it mocks it, misunderstands it and strikes it, is always wrong.

31 · The Battle of the Rue Gay Lussac

Two versions of the Battle of the Rue Gay Lussac fought on the night of Friday, 10 May 1968.

The Government Communiqué

From about 9 pm on several thousand demonstrators, gathered in the Place Edmond-Rostand and in the immediate vicinity, started digging up the cobblestones from the streets and building barricades.

After the failure of the attempts at peace-making the police were given the order, at 2.15 am, to disperse the demonstrators and to re-establish public order, which could no longer be flouted. This operation was carried out in conditions made very difficult by the fires lit by the demonstrators.

What is the meaning of the attitude of the young people who took part in the troubles of the recent days?

For some it is simply a question of imposing by means of violence their revolutionary convictions.

But the majority of them are expressing in an often blameworthy fashion a disquietude in the face of their professional future and a desire for the university to adapt itself.

The Government which has done much to these ends, knows that much is still to be done. It is ready to listen to all useful advice, including any that the students can give in a constructive spirit.

The offer made by the rector of the Sorbonne is still valid. The Government will continue its efforts so that the Sorbonne may be reopened in normal conditions and so that the reform of education can go forward in the interests of all.

32

Issued at the same time from the UNEF headquarters.

The UNEF Communiqué

Until the very end, the orders given by the UNEF were respected: peaceful occupation of the Quartier Latin, setting up of discussion groups, but also preparation for a possible détente. These orders were formal and were respected. The demonstrators were not to provoke any incidents. Deliberately at a quarter past two am the forces of order began to clear the Quartier. As well as the classical tear-gas grenades, the police used chlorine grenades, sulphur grenades, ammonia grenades and offensive grenades against the demonstrators. The Quartier Latin became the scene of incredible violence on the part of the police. The latter pursued the demonstrators even into buildings and this pursuit went on into the next morning. Moreover the police gave no help whatsoever to the first aid teams. On the contrary first aid workers were seen to be clubbed by police truncheons. The students and the worker must now take note of the replies given by the Government to the questions that they had put. For its part, the national headquarters of UNEF calls on all students to keep the strike going and not to yield to violence.

33 · The call for a general strike

A communiqué issued by the CGT and CFDT jointly at mid-day, 11 May 1968

The union organisations having appealed for a mass protest in the face of the grave events of the Quartier Latin met in emergency session on Saturday 11 May. They have decided to take up the challenge of the Government and to call for a general strike of 24 hours duration on Monday 13 May and for powerful demonstrations in which the population can and will participate massively. An end to repression, freedom, democracy! Long live the unity of workers and students!

34 · Press comment on the student insurrection

a) 'Le Figaro', 5 May 1968 (leading article)

Are these young people really students? They seem to be more like delinquents than members of a university. Are these really the adults that they want to be taken for? It is sickening to see how the thousand youths in revolt can bring the whole machine of the university to a halt.

b) 'Combat', 7 May 1968 (leading article)

Who is responsible? One man and one man alone, whose personal failure is quite evident: M. Jean Roche, rector of the university. In fact, M. Roche—because of fear? because of docility?—has provoked the legitimate anger of the students by giving the Sorbonne over to the police, by delivering the students who were there to the police as well, in spite of the promise he had made to them, and quite shamelessly. There is only one possible conclusion: because he panicked, because he has failed in his duty, because he has led thousands of students to the bludgeonings of the police, M. Roche must resign.

c) 'Le Parisien Liberé', 7 May 1968 (leading article)

The events of the last few weeks, which have seen nothing less than commandos organised in the 'Chinese' manner marching as on parade, prepared and equipped for rioting, and often led by foreign agitators, have not helped to inspire confidence in the students.

d) 'L'Aurore', 7 May 1968 (leading article)

However pointless Cohn-Bendit's slogans may be, however confused the arguments used by his supporters, however indefensible their behaviour, it must not be forgotten that this agitation is the hateful expression of a certain anxiety, an anxiety unfortunately justified by the rising generation when faced with the problems awaiting it.

e) 'L'Express', 13 May 1968

For three-quarters of a century lies have been told about 'the colonial Empire', which was at one and the same time an enterprise of repugnant oppression and a source of weakness for the country; lies have been told about the 'victory of 1918', which had been paid in a carnage so fearful that it involved the definitive decline of the nation; lies have been told about 'good government' by Poincaré and his like, who under the fallacious pretext of stability succeeded in weakening France by diminishing, incredible as it may seem, her industrial production between the two wars by 20 per cent; lies have been told about the 'popular front', which began by letting down the Spanish Republicans and which led France to Munich and ended up with Pétain; lies have been told about 'the Liberation', which instead of giving rise to a clear and passionate concern, after so many mistakes and tragedies, was used in fact as a springboard for colonial wars and the leukemia of inflation. Lies were told on the 6 February 1956[1], lies were told again on 13 May 1958[2]; and in 1968 lies are still being told on both sides when

[1] Date of Mollet's visit to Algiers and his surrender to the Colonial lobby.

[2] Date of de Gaulle's return to power.

people claim to be building political independence at the same time as they are abandoning the economic base of it to external colonisation; or when they still see in the Soviet bureaucracy of twenty years ago a way towards justice and prosperity.

After so many decades of lies, it is no longer possible to suggest a dialogue based on trust. The peasants, the miners, the postmen no longer believe what they are told; and less than anyone, the students do not believe it either. The question is no longer even the working out of reforms through free discussion, for the minimum necessary belief has been exhausted. The problem is now the problem of power.

6 · The Great Strike (14–26 May)

Chronology of the Crisis

Tuesday 14 May

De Gaulle leaves on a state visit to Rumania after announcing a TV broadcast for the 24th. Debate in the National Assembly on the events in the Quartier Latin and the crisis in the University. Pompidou presents an amnesty plan and concludes: 'I appeal for the cooperation of everyone, including the students'. The Left presents a motion of censure on the Government. Many faculties and high schools are occupied. The Sud Aviation factory at Nantes goes on strike and the workers occupy the factory and lock the manager in his office.

Wednesday 15 May

The Renault works at Cléon goes on strike. In Bordeaux, the France–Gironde shipyard goes on strike. The Odéon theatre in Paris is occupied and transformed into a permanent discussion centre. The demonstrators arrested or sentenced are released. Pompidou declares: 'Students will take part in the university reforms'. But examinations must be held as planned. Demonstration of 1,000 supporters of the extreme right-wing movement Occident at the Arc de Triomphe. The PCF warns against adventurism.

Thurday 16 May

The workers at the Renault works at Flins demonstrate, then call a sit-in strike which spreads quickly to the Renault factories at Le Mans and Billancourt. Many factories in other cities also go on strike. The students' slogan is: 'Boycott the exams'. Pompidou declares on TV: 'The Government will do its duty'.

Friday 17 May

The strike spreads to the public sector of industry. The central postal sorting office is occupied. The railway-men declare that they are joining in the strike. Students march to the Renault works at Billancourt. But the CGT shop stewards oppose all contacts with the students and do not allow them to enter the factory. 'Cohn-Bendit is playing Pompidou's game', declares the CGT.

Saturday 18 May

The railways, postal services and airlines go on strike. De Gaulle returns from Rumania earlier than expected.

Sunday 19 May

The strike has become a general strike de facto. At the Cabinet meeting de Gaulle declares: 'Yes to reforms. No to tom-foolery[1]'. The first CDR committees appear. After 24 hours of discussion the film festival at Cannes is closed down.

Monday 20 May

The strike spreads to all services and also to trade. In Paris the anxiety of the middle classes is made clear by long queues in

---

[1] He used the word 'chienlit', having a strong barrack-room flavour. It was much deplored.

front of the banks, at petrol stations, and food shops. In the National Assembly the Left demands the Government's resignation and fresh elections. The CFDT and the UNEF in a press conference held jointly declare: 'The struggle of the students and the workers is one struggle', but Séguy replies: 'No deviation and no insurrection'. The Paris stock-exchange ceases to quote share prices. Attacks by Occident on the Faculty of Political Science, on the Opéra and at St Lazare. Occupation of more high schools. Jean-Paul Sartre goes to the Sorbonne.

Tuesday 21 May   Opening of the censure debate at the National Assembly. Pisani, former Minister of Agriculture, votes in favour of the censure motion and then resigns together with another Gaullist deputy, René Capitant. In Brittany the workers make common cause with the peasants. There are student agitations in Belgium, Germany and England in solidarity with the French students. Cohn-Bendit in Berlin. Primary and High School teachers go on strike.

Wednesday 22 May   The motion of censure is defeated thanks to the support of Centre deputies. Cohn-Bendit, now in Amsterdam, is formally forbidden to return to France. L'Humanité defines him as 'A German Jew'. Ten thousand people demonstrate to protest against the ban on his return. Violent clashes at the Odéon. The CGT harshly criticises the 'incredible pretensions of the UNEF' and joins with the PCF in boycotting the demonstration. The staff in the big hotels in Paris go on strike. The petrol stations are closed. The amnesty law is approved. The strike is now general throughout France.

Thursday 23 May   New clashes with the police in the Quartier Latin; 200 arrested. De Gaulle goes on television to announce a referendum: he declares that he will resign if he does not have a complete majority.

Friday 24 May   The CGT organises a demonstration of protest separate from that of the UNEF, whilst the CFDT, FO and other union organisations join the students. It is the bloodiest of the battles of May. The Bourse is set on fire, and other fires are started in the city. Barricades are erected in the Quartier Latin. The police make no destinction between passers-by, demonstrators, the inhabitants of the Quartier, doctors and nurses attempting to aid the many wounded. Later, in the police stations there are further scenes of violence against the people arrested, including the wounded. Official figures speak of 500 wounded and 800 arrested. But wounded probably number over 1,000. Two deaths: a police officer at Lyons crushed by a runaway lorry, and a demonstrator in Paris on the barricades. Although the CGT exhorts the workers not to take part in the student demonstration, many do. About 100,000 people involved in the demonstrations in Paris. Peasants demonstrate in the provinces, especially in the west of France. Violent riots in the provinces at Nantes, Bordeaux, and Lyons. The banks are closed. The ORTF staff go on strike.

Saturday 25 May   In Rue Grenelle, at the Ministry of Social Security, negotiations begin between Government, employers and unions. Pompidou states: 'The demonstrators will be dispersed with the maximum energy!' André Barjonet, CGT economics expert, resigns from PCF and joins the PSU.

Sunday 26 May   The negotiations at Rue Grenelle seem to end with what the CGT declares to be 'a draft agreement'. The Ministry of the Interior declares that the 'criminal world' is taking part in the demonstrations.

35 · How the strike hit Arras

This description of the situation in Arras is typical of the way schoolchildren, workers, teachers and administrators in the provinces reacted to the May Events.

**'The Times',
20 May 1968**

The school system of Arras, capital of the Pas-de-Calais department, disintegrated today in a series of spontaneous eruptions that left five schools occupied by teenagers with the full support of their disgruntled teachers.

Early today the boys' *lycée* was taken over by a mass of pupils who announced that they would occupy it indefinitely. Plans were being made this evening for a permanent 'sleep-in'. Many of the 1,000 pupils were milling round the modern buildings of the school today, organizing theatre shows, nailing up banners, and discussing educational reform with their teachers.

Teachers and students, who claim almost unanimous support, have formed a joint committee to arrange discussions about how the schools should be run. They were in permanent session this afternoon in a smoke-filled room on the top floor of the building, and a teacher came out to announce that support among teachers had been virtually total.

About noon the boys, led by an 18-year-old philosophy student, carried the torch of educational revolt to the girls' *lycée* up the road. In a few hours placards announcing 'total occupation' were up outside the school which houses 1,500 girls. The teachers went over in a body and all work stopped.

Within hours three other schools or training colleges had been occupied, and news arrived that the revolt in secondary education was spreading like a plague across France.

'We are not against de Gaulle or Pompidou, or anyone in particular', an 18-year-old girl told me. 'We're against the Government.' A boy insisted there was no political background to the dispute; a claim borne out by the absence of Maoist and other literature that is piled high in the Sorbonne courtyard at Paris.

The students in Arras limit their demands to educational reform. They want more sensible examinations, smaller classes, and better courses. Ironically, all are housed in buildings which are luxurious by British standards.

In a well-appointed lecture hall this afternoon 18-year-old girl students, teachers, and parents debated passionately about reform of the baccalaureate, trying to decide whether to refuse to sit for the examination. (M. Pompidou, the Prime Minister, has already announced that the examinations will not be delayed.)

In a new secondary school on the outskirts of Arras, teachers refused to give lessons and chatted with their 16-year-old pupils throughout the day. 'We want reform', said a pretty young teacher of English, 'smaller classes, and less centralization'. A French teacher said that, in the absence of orders from the teachers' unions, they had gone ahead this morning with their plan of refusing to teach. Pupils are to meet tomorrow morning to present a list of demands for reform to the headmaster.

The headmaster was a much shaken man when we saw him in his almost deserted school this afternoon. After ritual denials of any trouble, he said boldly: 'I don't know what happened in the classrooms. I do not know, and I don't want to know.'

A young National Service man in the street asked if he would fire on students or workers, replied: 'Never. I think their methods are a bit rough, but I am a worker's son myself.'

The workers of Arras are keeping clear of the students today, but if anything they are more radical. Outside the grimy Arras-Maxei metallurgical works the local representative of the communist-led trade union told me: 'We keep apart from the students but we don't criticize one another. *On ne se mange pas le nez.*'

A crowd of workers barred all but the manager from this factory, which along with several others in Arras has been occupied all day by workers after a vote on the site. 'We want a change of government', the group's leader said. 'If Pompidou goes, we'll work.'

The police in Arras are keeping well out of sight, and only the occasional rumbling of an Army lorry drawing a field-gun strikes a menacing note. The city authorities appear paralysed, waiting for decisions from above.

Perhaps they remember that it was a little lawyer from Arras called Robespierre who less than 200 years ago successfully challenged another autocracy.

36 · How the strike affected France

'The Economist',
25 May 1968

By Thursday, strikes were almost completely paralysing the French economy; 8 million workers, about half the total of wage and salary earners, are on strike; there are no trains, no metro (though worse traffic jams have been seen in other French crises), foreign airliners land only in good weather with no help from ground staff. The newspapers are still being published but only after anxious daily debates on how and if they can be distributed. The strikes are not restricted to previously well-unionised factories like Renault. They have spread to companies like Citroën and Dassault, which formerly had only tame company unions or none at all. The Banque de France has struck solidly—only 50 people are being allowed in by the pickets. This has meant troubles in the distribution of bank notes to the banks most of which have closed anyway. On Wednesday, the workers at petrol depots started to strike, which must eventually immobilise private cars. But for the moment life is surprisingly normal: there is still food in the shops, and petrol for sale (at least to favoured customers).

When it came to Ascension Day, a large part of the country, whether officially on strike or not, used the public holiday as an excuse for a day, and possibly a long week-end in the country.

The atmosphere is curious; not the fear that was all pervasive ten years ago in the weeks before the General came to power, but an exhilaration, an uncertainty if this is revolution or a jolly little revolt. Paris is, as usual, more revolutionary than the provinces, with a few exceptions. Lyons has a lot of strikes and the situation in Brittany could be very serious. There the traditionally communist workers in the shipyards at St Nazaire are being joined by the discontented Breton nationalists and peasants in a giant and much-feared demonstration on Friday. In this fluid state, what may save French capitalism is the major union group, the communist Confédération Générale du Travail. It has been a reluctant follower of the students and the more impatient workers. It hopes to make rather limited gains out of the situation; increased wages, shorter working hours, increased minimum pay, and, most significant of all, official union recognition and representation in companies which had previously been its most adamant opponents. Those companies may relent, because the alternative is so awful. The managements may welcome the call by M. Séguy, head of the CGT, for a grand round-table conference of workers, employers and the government. The alternative is the vague, ill-defined, but solid anti-capitalism emanating not just from the students, but from left-wing Catholic intellectuals both outside and in the other major trade union federation, the Confédération Française Democratique du Travail.

Curiously enough, though, General de Gaulle and his finance minister M. Debré share, in a very watered-down form, some of these ideas—which in their more extreme forms are trotskyite or maoist. The famous Vallon amendement gave expression to a gaullist dream of an organic society transcending capitalism in uniting in a 'pan-capitalist' society workers, state, employers and shareholders. So it will not be too difficult for the president or M. Debré to make some gestures towards this feeling of revulsion against traditional capitalism.

37 · The Grenelle agreement

a) This letter, addressed to the management side by the workers on strike at an oil refinery is typical of the bargaining positions assumed at plant level by most union negotiators during the general strike. Note the combination of 'social' (1 & 2) and 'industrial' (3–14) demands.

Following conversations with the staff during this week's strike, we have modified the demands we made on the 19 May last. You will find the altered list below:

1 Repeal of the regulations concerning social security.
2 Extension of union rights.
   (a) Freedom of action for union organisations within industry:

collection of subscriptions, distribution of press and union literature, staff meetings and assemblies during working hours.

(*b*) Application of article 2 of the law of 18 June 1966 concerning the social attributions of the worker-management committee, the text to be modified in the following way:

the worker-management committee participates with the management, instead of cooperating.

the committee *decides* what use to make of the 1 per cent contribution out of salaries.

the committee *decides on solutions* to general problems concerning professional training and finishing.

(*c*) Application of article 3 of the law of 16 May 1946, which concerns the economic role of the worker-management committee, the phrase '*on a consultative basis*' being abolished.

3 Basic oil unit at 3·85 francs.

4 A 40-hour week with no reduction in salary.

5 Retirement at 60 years of age. For posted wage-earners or those working in particularly unpleasant or unhealthy conditions, retiring age should be put forward, with the same advantages as for other workers, in terms of one year for every three years spent engaged in this work. This clause cannot make it possible for those concerned to be fully retired before the age of 55.

6 The 5th week of paid holidays.

7 Abolition of fines for delay in the performance of a contract.

8 Immediate engagement of staff on a contract basis.

9 Compensatory bonus (increased to 150 Fr.).

10 Indexing of the housing bonus.

11 Watch and seniority bonuses to be calculated in terms of real income.

12 Planning of relief timetables (teams to be made up in such a way that any unforeseen absences in the relief team should not lead to anyone having to stay at his post; guarantees of employment, classification and wages when a worker who is usually on shift or semi-shift work has to do a normal day because he is directed to, or for personal reasons).

13 Professional training.

14 Remuneration of days lost during the current strike.

b) The terms and implications of the Grenelle agreement.

'The Economist'

1 June 1968

Monday morning's offer is still significant in that it had employers (and a conservative government) making concessions which had been obstinately refused in the course of the preceding months and years. The concessions they gave were that

1 Take-home pay was to go up on June 1st by 7 per cent, including any increases given since the beginning of the year, with a further 3 per cent on 1 October this year. At the same time discussions were going on in different nationalised industries. Only the coalminers had accepted the government propositions; and because of the political situation, they have not yet gone back to work as was foreseen.

2 In March, 1969, unions and employers would meet to discuss the trend of the buying power of wages. The CGT has asked for something much more important that wage increases should be linked to price increases, thus presumably perpetuating the spiral for ever.

3 The working week would be gradually reduced to 40 hours without loss of wages, according to a time scale negotiated separately in each profession. But in any case before the end of 1969, the working week would be reduced by two hours when it was more than 48 hours or one hour when it was between 45 and 48 hours.

4 Various concessions were given in the spheres of family allowances, pensions and social security benefits. But the prime minister refused the demands of the CGT (which has not abandoned the attempt) to withdraw last August's decrees reforming the social security system.

5 M. Malterre (a former supporter of Algérie Française), speaking in the name of the cadres got concessions in the system of direct taxes.

6 Last and most important, the unions got what they have been demanding for a long time: recognition of union activity within company organisation.

Scattered through most of the occupied factories, some workers have been demanding a share in running the companies involved. These workers, most often belong to the Christian-Socialist Confédération Française du Travail. The communist CGT says that this idea is a futile one.

c) The workers say 'No' to Séguy and reject the Grenelle agreement.

The 'New Statesman', 31 May 1968

For on Monday morning at Billancourt, in the courtyard of the biggest factory in France—Renault—I watched a pathetic drama. Benoît Frachon, the veteran chieftain of the communist trade unionists, was there to stand beside Séguy his successor, and thus lend a solemn air to the meeting which—as at the end of the great 1936 strike—was supposed to endorse new agreements between the workers, the employers and the government. But, although Renault is a CGT stronghold, Séguy couldn't have found a worse place to announce the outline agreements reached the night before with Pompidou. The one serious concession made by the government was to raise the national minimum wage by 35 per cent. But at Renault it is many years since anyone had to live off this minimum, so no one had reason to cheer. As soon as Séguy announced that the workers would only get half-pay for the strike period, and moreover would have to work off this payment in overtime, a loud and unanimous 'No' came from 20,000 voices. Séguy could only shout 'Comrades, we haven't signed yet. We're not going to sign.' At the end of his speech, when he tried to issue a warning against the 'provocateurs' and 'irresponsible elements' of the student movement, it fell completely flat. No one clapped, and even the most loyal CGT followers must have known in their hearts that the 'irresponsible elements' had sized the situation up right. They declared that it was no good negotiating with a government incapable of meeting the demands of the hour. In 1936 fewer than 3 million strikers won concessions that were revolutionary for that period: four weeks' paid holiday, collective bargaining, the 40-hour week. In 1968, with 9 million on strike, the CGT has won nothing that could bring about a qualitative change in the French workers' life. Even in the field of social security it agreed to have the problems debated in parliament, a forum more discredited today than ever in history. They say in France 'as Renault goes, the working class go'. Predictably, every major factory turned down the agreement within a few hours. One could only wonder how the CGT could have failed to foresee the outcome of its confrontation with the rank and file.

That afternoon in the Charléty stadium, 50,000 students and young workers gathered to join in the slogans of the UNEF (students' union): 'de Gaulle Out! The fight goes on!' But they also shouted 'Séguy out!' and 'CP Betrayal'. Among the speakers were leaders of the formerly Catholic and socialist trade union movements, as well as André Barjonet, who had just resigned as a CGT official. Never before has the CP been so visibly outflanked on its left; never has it had to deal with a young revolutionary movement totally outside its control.

38 · The occupation of the Odéon
(Seale and McConville)

Two days after the occupation of the Sorbonne on 13 May a column of students took over one of Paris' National Theatres, the Odéon. In terms of publicity it quickly turned sour because of student exhibitionism.

The occupation of the Odéon was a baroque unmeditated gesture, a flourish on the margin of the revolution, not part of the main stream. It was inspired by Cohn-Bendit's 22 March Movement, according to the spontaneous strategy he advocated, without consultation with the more hard-headed groups which made up the revolutionary leadership.

In the month of its occupation the 'ex-Théâtre de France' was open day and night as a sort of revolutionary forum, club and doss house. No plays were put on but countless wordy, marathon debates. It was an experiment denounced by the students' union, UNEF, as well as by the French Actors' Union. As the days passed, groups of squatters came and went, plundering the wardrobes for theatrical costumes, and thus confronting the police in the street skirmishes with an army of extras. A tramp made his home in this temple of direct democracy, rising from time to time to intervene in the debates from his seat in the gallery. *'Eh ben,'* he croaked one evening, 'I've been here five nights, and I must say I'm very happy. Every morning I go and buy my litre of red, and then I bed down. *Eh ben*, I must say I'm very happy.' (Applause.) At the end there was a hard core of about a hundred, living and sleeping and cooking in the theatre, sunbathing on the roof, strutting about as Roman centurions, more like a gang of teddy-boys on leave from the street corner and the vacant lot. When the police came on 14 June, they all left quietly, giving way to the DDT cleaning squads.

39 · The strike at the ORTF

The 'Guardian', 30 May 1968

Throughout Paris there are posters of a man with a microfilm in his hand and a gag in his mouth. Written across it is the slogan 'Information Libre.'

Most of the journalists working for ORTF, the French radio and television, are trying to get rid of that gag and make sure that in future the claim to have freedom and objectivity of speech in their news media will be a statement of fact and not the cause of derision.

For General de Gaulle—and equally for his successors—to concede control over radio and television would be a crucial political decision, and will not be easily made. Meanwhile, however, the General has already effectively lost control over the sound news services and, to a lesser extent, even over television news.

The radio journalists are technically on strike, but are occupying the handsome Maison de la Radio, have ousted their directors, and are working without pay putting out long and full news bulletins going far beyond anything their audience has been getting in the past. Between news times, they put on records for the listeners (all other radio programmes are off because of the strike) and, with their colleagues from the television news, they spend the time hammering out a new charter for ORTF.

All French television matters are less clear-cut. All services except the news stopped more than a week ago. The news programmes however, one at midday and two in the evening, continued virtually unchanged until last Saturday, though there were stormy meetings between reporters trying to break out of their straitjackets and the programme director seeking to maintain the old pattern and barely allowing even any eyewitness reporting of the street battles in the Latin Quarter.

Then, on Saturday evening 116 of the 150 television journalists voted to strike after the directors had refused for the third time to let them carry M. Waldeck Rochet's and M. Gaston Defferre's comments on General de Gaulle's speech on Friday. The strikers were, however, in no position to occupy the studio and operate the news programmes themselves as 44 of their colleagues voted against the strike and decided to present one news programme a day.

The technicians of the studio gave warning that they would allow the news to go out only if it was impartial. It is coming out on day-to-day sufferance and has been of poor and timid quality. The Government, however, has under its control a studio in the Eiffel Tower, where a programme could be put out if the remaining technicians at the ORTF studios decide to strike.

The French Government's control of radio and television news has long been notorious. It is not a Gaullist phenomenon alone. It goes back at least 20 years, but General de Gaulle did not hesitate to use the two media for his own purposes. There is no doubt that television especially has been used as a major propaganda instrument for him.

At television the control has been more blatant and the wonder is that so many of its reporters who are now so vehemently fighting for a new charter put up with it for so long. Invisible to them, but allegedly watching them nightly, was the General himself, making sure his policies were being given adequate television coverage—and soon letting it be known when his displeasure was aroused.

Day-to-day control on behalf of the Government was maintained by a committee which met every morning. On it sat representatives from the major Ministries, who indicated which item of news deserved major coverage and which should best be ignored. If nothing else, this produced a situation where foreign news coverage, especially where it affected the General's policy objectives, was consistently given far lengthier attention than domestic news.

40 · Pompidou's warning:

Text of the broadcast address, 16 May 1968

Frenchmen, Frenchwomen:

I have given proof of my desire for peace. With the agreement of the President of the Republic, who will address you in a few days, I have held out my hand to them for the broadest and most constructive cooperation.

I have freed the arrested demonstrators. I have announced a total amnesty. My appeals have not been heeded at all. Groups of enraged ones—we have shown some of them [Mr Pompidou's speech followed a panel discussion between three young extremist leaders and journalists]—propose to make the disorder general, with the avowed goal of destroying the nation and the very foundations of our free society.

Frenchmen, Frenchwomen:

The Government must defend the Republic—it will defend it.

I address myself to you with calm but with gravity.

Students, do not follow the provocateurs who declare themselves unconcerned with three-quarters of you. Listen to the voice of reason. We are ready to hear all your legitimate demands. Do not ruin them by excesses.

Frenchmen, Frenchwomen:

It is up to you to show, by your coolness, but also by your resolution, whatever be your political preferences, whatever be your social demands, that you reject anarchy.

The Government will do its duty. It asks you to help it.

41 · How the strike spread: a factory worker's account

A young worker at the Renault works at Flins tells how the strike spread

There had already been a stoppage for two hours the previous day, when we heard that Cléon had gone on strike.

On the morning of 16 May the shop stewards came round the workshops to tell us we were downing tools at 10.15. We found ourselves outside, about two, three hundred of us; the shop stewards asked us to go back into the workshops to get the others to come out as well. We already knew that Cléon had stopped the previous day—they send us the engines, and we only have half a day's engines in advance to work with. We went back to the production lines until midday to explain things to the blokes; we went back again later in the afternoon, for the people on shift-work, and by the evening there were more than 8,000 of us outside, out of perhaps 10,500 in all. We started to get organised and to enrol blokes in the strike pickets and I spent the first night there; I spent at least seven other nights there afterwards, there must have been about eight strike pickets in the whole factory; there were rounds from one gate to another, guard duties etc. We could go into the yard, in the corridors, the changing rooms, but not in the workshops. At the beginning the watches were too long, but afterwards we soon got organised with turns on watch of four hours on, four hours off.

42 · Schoolboys on strike: two leaflets

These were distributed in Lyon by High School activists (CAL)

THE LYCEE COMMITTEE wants the administration officially to:
recognise the elected committee
allow it the use of some rooms
reserve part of the notice board for its needs
allow people from outside the *lycée* to be invited to rooms reserved to pupils
admit pupil participation in the internal and disciplinary councils of the *lycée*

Furthermore, the Committee wants pupil-teacher commissions to be set up to examine the following problems:

pedagogy and teaching
courses
timetables
teaching methods
exams
careers
guidance
teacher-pupil relations

THE COMMITTEE

Monday 20 May

LET US FIGHT:
1 For the creation of a schoolboy 'Union'.
2 For the revision of courses which are overloaded and not adapted to working life.
3 To solve the universities' and techs' selection problem.
4 For a new type of exam.
   Quadripartite management of schools by:
   Administration, teaching staff, parents, pupils.
5 To secure job openings following success or failure in the technical and ordinary '*bacs*'.
6 For better psycho-pedagogic training of teaching staff.
7 To alter the character of lessons.
8 For a more appropriate syllabus.
9 For the pupils' rights to be represented at teachers' meetings.
10 For the inclusion of civic training in lectures.

43 · Resignation statement of André Barjonet

André Barjonet, for 20 years the leading economics expert of the CGT resigned on 23 May and made this statement to 'Le Combat'.

'I have resigned from my duties at the CGT, duties which I have carried out for almost 22 years and you will therefore very easily understand that for me it was a crisis of conscience. I did it for two main reasons. The first is that I have not only the conviction but the certainty that the leadership of the CGT has no intention of leading this formidable movement in a direction which is likely to bring about political changes in society.

'But in the face of a movement which brings together the working class and the student world, which has stirred people from all walks of life, it is unforgivable not to have acted. For years the CGT has never missed an opportunity for saying to the workers that one must get rid of Gaullism and move towards Socialism. For years we have never hidden the fact that our aim in the CGT was not only defence of your interests but also, and above all, to get rid of the power of monopoly of the Gaullist regime. Then when the time was ripe . . . Georges Séguy gets up and makes a speech declaring that the CGT does not intend to go beyond day-to-day Union demands.

'The second reason, less fundamental than the first but certainly not unimportant, concerns the scornful attitude of the Secretary General, Georges Séguy towards the student movement. I do not necessarily approve of methods the students have used or indeed of Daniel Cohn-Bendit. But Séguy's attitude seems to me to be wrong.

'I think we have come near to the Socialist Revolution. If one had put the question in France barely two months ago as to whether our country was ripe for Socialism one would have laughed or sighed. We thought only in terms of Parliamentary change. From now on the question of Revolution is on the agenda. As Karl Marx wrote, "When an idea takes hold of the masses it becomes a material force".'

44 · Speeches made in the censure debate 22–23 May 1968

a) Robert Poujade, Secretary of the UDR.

a) The thesis of certain representatives of the Opposition, according to which the troubles at Nanterre can be explained by the incapacity of the Government to foresee the needs of the university and to provide for them, does not correspond to reality in the least.

There are many things to be revised in the university, that is certain. The isolation of the student is the deep cause of the dramatic days which we have lived through. Is that the same as saying that everything will be solved by the romantic parody we have seen of the October days? Can people imagine that there will be no more exams? Would you entrust your children to teachers whose capacity had never been examined?

I have just returned from Dijon, and I can tell you that the great majority of the workers do not stop work with any enthusiasm and spontaneity. The scenario is the same everywhere: the minority sets up pickets, and thus resolves the problem of the right to work, and the firm is closed down.

The right to strike is a real right and is sometimes a duty: only countries without freedom have no strikes. But in this month of May 1968, the French workers are undergoing the strike more than deciding on it.

b) François Mitterrand

b) We have decided to claim the responsibility of taking power in order to bring about an alliance between the fighters for individual liberty and the fighters for collective liberty, the fighters for Socialism and the fighters for freedom.

In the name of Socialism it is necessary to change policies. In the name of liberty it is necessary to sweep away the exceptions to the law, to reform the teaching profession and to liberalise the flow of information. In the immediate future, only a Left majority will be able to give back hope to those who are engaged in the struggle. Only a government of the Left would be able to create a wide current of reconciliation. . . .

Where is the popular consensus on which you have founded your legitimacy? Just go outside this building and you will see!

Starting from the unity of the Left and the republicans who will join it we will form a government which will not be a government of rancour but a government of national unity. But first of all, and I say this very seriously, Mr Prime Minister, first of all you must go.

c) Georges Pompidou

c) The Government knows what conclusions to draw from the facts. Events of this importance, even if they have occurred suddenly in a way which has surprised everybody, cannot but have deep causes. Afterwards nothing can ever be the same again. It is obvious that when trade union organisations, taking up the demands of the workers, show that they have such a wide following, there can be no Government able to ignore them—which of course we have never done. . . . I am therefore ready to undertake a dialogue with all the trades union organisations, I am ready to call them together. For the Government it is a question of finding out from all the trade union organisations precisely and completely what they are looking for. If they wish to obtain the satisfaction of a certain numbers of demands, then all demands can be examined and discussed. . . . It is clear that such discussions cannot be carried on and concluded unless the demands are free of political implications, from insurrectional implications. For insurrection is not only a question of taking up arms and going into the streets, it is also attempting through the pressure of the streets to prevent the normal functioning of institutions and the normal expression of the will of the citizens.

d) Giscard d'Estaing

d) Finally we are concerned about the nature of the support which the Government will receive and accept. It is in effect that of the party of fear, which is numerous in times of trouble, fickle when reassured and which has never been the party of reform. To depend on its support is to risk becoming one day a member of the tribe of those who, in the words of Goethe, prefer injustice to disorder. Several speakers have stated that many Frenchmen, in all classes of society, fear disorder. That may be, but that does not mean that they approve the old order.

45 · PCF Communiqués 16–25 May 1968

16 May 1968

We are witnessing the explosion of discontent which has accumulated during ten years because of the Gaullist Government which has been in charge of the country and which has run it for the capitalist monopolies against the working-class and all the non-monopoly social classes, and against the present and future interests of the French nation. . . .

Agreement among the parties of the Left on a social programme which goes beyond the stage reached on 24 February and provides the basis of a majority programme is now becoming urgent. The politburo of the PCF renews its proposals of unity to the FGDS in this regard.

The Politburo warns the workers and students against any adventurist slogan—particularly on the occasions of demonstrations which it has not itself helped to organise—which may hinder the development of a movement of unequalled breadth, which is necessary so as to put an end to the power of the monopolies and to make democracy triumph.

20 May 1968

It is not possible, without risking disappointing the people's hopes, to pose the problem of a change of Government without laying down precisely its basis of action, *i.e.:*

1 Satisfaction of the fundamental demands of the working-class:
  (a) abrogation of the August Social Security cuts;
  (b) general increase in wages;
  (c) reduction in working hours;
  (d) recognition of trade union rights in factories and the extension of works councils' powers.

2 Satisfaction of the basic demand of teachers and students: reform of the university by the university itself.

The common objective of all the forces wishing to construct the future of France is therefore clear. The great masses of the people, whose action is decisive, are not engaged either in a re-shuffle of the existing autocratic government nor in an insurrectionary strike, but in a vast movement whose purpose is to get rid of both the Government and the régime of Gaullism and to bring about, together with all the forces of the Left, a real republican régime which will open the way to Socialism.

25 May 1968

At this moment of profound crisis of the Gaullist régime, the Politburo underlines that the political formations claiming to represent the working-class and democracy have a duty to work out without any further delays and excuses the common programme which it will be their job to carry out together after the elimination of the Gaullist system. The lack of such an agreement is contributing to the survival of the existing Government. This is why the Politburo proposes an immediate meeting between the Communist Party, the FGDS and the union leaderships with the aim of working out and rapidly adopting a programme which would give moreover a real meaning to the demand for a dissolution of the National Assembly and fresh elections.

46 · De Gaulle's television speech 24 May 1968

'Everyone understands, obviously, the significance of the present events—university, and now social.

'There is to be seen in them all the signs which show the necessity of a mutation of our society, and everything indicates that this mutation should include a more extensive participation of everyone in the conduct and result of the activities which directly concern them.

'Certainly, in the upset situation of today the first duty of the state is to ensure, in spite of everything, the primary existence of the country, and public order as well. It is doing that. Its duty is also to help getting things going again, notably by making the contacts which could facilitate this. It is ready for this.

'So much for the immediate situation. But after that we shall have to, without any doubt, modify structures, that is, make reforms.

'Because if, in the immense political, economic and social transformation which France is accomplishing in our time, many internal and external obstacles already have been overcome, others still stand in our way. From this come the deep disturbances, primarily among youth which is concerned about its own role and is too often worried about the future.

'That is why the crisis in the university, a crisis caused by the impotence of that great institution to adapt itself to the modern needs of the nation, and at the same time to the role and the proper occupation of young people, has by contagion unleashed in many other places a tidal wave of disorders or of surrenders or of work stoppages.

'The result is that our country is at the edge of paralysis. Facing ourselves and facing the work, we Frenchmen must settle the essential problem which our epoch asks of us. Otherwise we will drift through civil war to the most odious and most ruinous adventures and usurpations.

'For nearly 30 years the events have imposed upon me, on several grave occasions, the duty of bringing our country around to assuming its own destiny in order to prevent others from doing it in spite of the country.

'I am ready this time, too, but, this time and especially this time, I need—yes, I need—the French people to say what they want. Now, our constitution provides exactly the way to do it. It is the most direct and most democratic way possible: the way of the referendum.

'Taking into account the completely exceptional situation in which we are, I have therefore, on the proposal of the Cabinet, decided to submit to the vote of the nation a proposed law in which I will ask the nation to give to the state and, above all, to the chief of state a mandate for renewal.

'The University is to be rebuilt, not according to its age-old habits but according to the real needs of the evolution of the country and of the actual job opportunities of the students in a modern society.

'The economy is to be adapted, not to one or another category of private interests but to the national and international needs of the present time, by improving the conditions of the life and work of the personnel in the public services and industry, by organizing their participation in professional responsibilities, by developing the training of youth, by assuring them jobs, by starting up industrial and agricultural activities according to the needs of our different regions.

'This is the goal which the whole nation should set for itself.

'Frenchwomen, Frenchmen, in the month of June you will decide by your votes. In case your reply is 'No', it is self-evident that I will not much longer remain in my office. If by a massive vote of 'Yes' you express your confidence in me, I will undertake with the agencies of the Government—and I hope the co-operation of all those who want to serve the common interest—to change, wherever necessary, structures which are narrow and out-dated, and to open the road more broadly to the new blood of France.

'Long live the Republic. Long live France.'

47 · The Opposition reacts to de Gaulle's referendum

a) François Mitterrand (FGDS)

a) After ten years of uncontrolled government, after a year of emergency powers exercised by means of decrees, after fifteen days of chaos and impotence, the Head of State finds no other solution to the crisis for which he is responsible but the reinforcement of his power. What sadness and anger are felt when one is faced by this derisory reply to the demands of our people and aspirations of our youth. The Federation of the Left says no to the plebiscite and no to General de Gaulle.

b) Pierre Mendès-France (PSU)

b) One does not discuss a plebiscite, one fights it. The people have already said no. They will not wait until June to reject this proposition.

Already the struggle is on a political level and is moving in a perfectly obvious direction.

c) Waldeck Rochet (PCF)

c) Negotiations with the trade union organisations are about to open: what millions of strikers and their families expect is the rapid satisfaction of their basic demands. But on the political level the problem of power is still the main problem. The Gaullist régime has had its day. It must go.

I stress that the Communists are not proposing structural reforms in order to bury under Leftist phraseology the essential demands of the workers such as a rise in wages, the progressive reduction of working hours, the withdrawal of the cuts in welfare services, and full employment for all.

Contrary to the statements of certain anarchist-type organisations these demands are not out-of-date: they must be satisfied without delay.

In order to have a complete change of policy and bring about genuine reforms of structure, an end must be put to the power of the monopolies and the power of the Gaullist régime, and a people's government must be promoted with the support of the will of the people.

The Communist Party which is ready to take its place in such a Government has not stopped proposing to other parties of the Left and to other democratic organisations an agreement on the basis of a common programme. It is not our fault if this agreement has not yet been realised.

48 · Draft text of the referendum

The text of the draft law on educational, social and economic reform to be put to the people in the referendum proposed for 16 June 1968

In order to extend participation of the citizens in the decisions concerning them directly all measures will be taken before 1 June 1969, by the President of the Republic, the Government and

Parliament within the framework of the respective competence of these public bodies and with the assistance of all representative organisations to:

1. Reform national education by adapting teaching and training of the young to the evolution and to the needs of the country and have those concerned in the transformation and the functioning of universities and other educational establishments participate therein as a whole.

2. Adapt the economic and administrative structures and promote social progress according to the national or international necessities by:

The distribution of the benefits of expansion with a view toward continuing improvement of standards of living and of working conditions in industrial enterprises, agriculture and public services, principally in so far as the least favoured social categories are concerned.

The participation of the workers in professional responsibilities and at all levels of the economy.

The drive toward full employment and professional training.

The organization of economic activity within the regional framework with the increased participation of the locally elected bodies and the trade union and professional organizations and the decentralization and deconcentration of administrations.

49 · Press comment on the Great Strike

In this comment on the student revolt Yuri Zhukov shows that for the Soviet communists the immediate enemy was on the left.

a) 'Pravda', 28 May 1968

Intensively played up in the bourgeois press nowadays are the 'escapades' of a certain Cohn-Bendit, a 23-year-old German from the Federal Republic, who until recently was a student at the Paris University where he occupied himself with splitting activities on the campus. Currently he is touring Western Europe with calls for a 'bloody revolution.'

Blasphemously using Marx's name, the werewolves, attempting to carry out the 'decommunisation of Marxism,' to split progressive forces and to place them at loggerheads, are thus fulfilling a most definite assignment of the enemies of the working class movement who are seriously alarmed over the intensification of the class struggle in their countries.

Unconcerned by de Gaulle's referendum the New China News Agency continued to beat its anti-Soviet drums as hard as ever.

b) New China News Agency, 27 May 1968

Openly siding with the French ruling class, the Soviet revisionist renegade clique has echoed the French monopoly capitalist class; it has exerted itself to the utmost to scurrilously vilify the French people's just struggle as 'riots', 'rebellious actions' and 'provocative demonstrations.' It viciously described the French students, who raised high their red banners in the demonstrations, as 'a small group of wild men,' 'hooligans' and 'irresponsible, confused and excited elements' who have been divorced from the masses, and so on and so forth. In so doing, it beats the drums for the French ruling class in its ruthless suppression of the revolutionary people.

The New York Times took a sceptical view of the chances of de Gaulle's referendum proposal.

c) 'The New York Times', 25 May 1968

Will the manoeuvre work? Does de Gaulle's personality still retain enough power so these vague promises and this obvious stalling for time will be enough to send workers back to their labor and students back to their studies? Yesterday's continued disorders were not bright auguries, but the real test comes today when union and Government representatives meet to discuss worker demands.

No doubt the referendum will be so ingeniously worded as to try to persuade Frenchmen that a vote for de Gaulle is a vote for France, for its prosperity, peace and greatness. This has always been the general's tactic; but the millions of striking students, workers and farmers have been suggesting that they no longer necessarily identify the power of de Gaulle with the interests of the nation. The President asked yesterday for a 'massive "yes",' but it is quite possible that the recent events really constitute a 'massive "no"' and—however Premier Pompidou's negotiations and the referendum turn out— mark the end of the era of de Gaulle's personal mastery of France.

'The Times', commenting on the same proposal took an even gloomier view of Gaullist prospects.

d) The Times, 25 May 1968

Probably—almost certainly— President de Gaulle missed the point in his broadcast last night. This is that a large mass of Frenchmen no longer believe that de Gaulle and his obedient Ministers can meet or even understand the demands that the strikers and the students are making. The message at the end of de Gaulle's speech was simple and challenging, but it was also unconvincing. Vote for me (he said, in effect) and I will lead you in a new direction.

Even in these vague terms this proposal is unlikely to convince. For 10 years de Gaulle has enjoyed the unfettered power to lead France in any direction new or old. The choice of direction has been his. To promise now to lead his country towards different goals is to confess that the old ones—chosen by de Gaulle— were wrong.

Whether the Government knows what to do in the situation is still dangerously unclear, even after yesterday's broadcast. A great many Frenchmen obviously now want de Gaulle to go. M. Mitterrand, who has kept a cool head throughout, suggested yesterday that this was the only possible solution. De Gaulle must go or disorder will continue. De Gaulle, M. Mitterrand said, 'must understand that it is all over and that peace in France comes before the final political manoeuvre which he is preparing.'

7 · The Political Arena (27–30 May)

**Chronology of the
Crisis**

Monday 27 May

The second week of strikes is now beginning involving over ten million workers. The workers of the Renault factories at Billancourt, followed by those of the Citroën, Berliet, Rhodiacète, Sud Aviation factories, etc. refuse the agreements made by the unions and decide to go on with the strike. Séguy denies that he has signed any agreement. The Cabinet approves the draft law for the referendum fixed for the 16 June. At Charléty Stadium the UNEF, FEN and PSU organise a mass-meeting. The CGT does not take part and at the same time organises a dozen rival demonstrations in Paris. 35,000 people meet at Charléty. Those taking part include Mendès-France, the CFDT, the FO, Barjonet, and two other officials of the CGT.

Tuesday 28 May

Mitterrand announces his candidature for the Presidency should the referendum go against de Gaulle and appeals to Mendès-France to be his Prime Minister. Representatives of the revolutionary Left, including Barjonet, Pierre Vigier (just expelled from the PCF), Alain Geismar (just resigned from SNE Sup.), Alain Krivine (JCR), a representative of the Mouvement du 22 mars, all meet to prepare the constitution of a revolutionary party. Pompidou declares: 'In order to allow the referendum to take place order must be restored'. The Minister of Education, Peyrefitte, resigns. The PCF and CGT call for a 'People's Government of Democratic Unity'. Cohn-Bendit, who has secretly returned to France, speaks at the Sorbonne during the evening. The first wage-settlement (in mining) announced.

Wednesday 29 May

De Gaulle disappears for 5 hours, then arrives at Colombey after a secret meeting in Germany with military leaders, headed by General Massu. The PCF and the CGT organise a demonstration in which the CAL, the Mouvement du 22 mars, and the Maoists take part; the participation of the UNEF is not official, but students are there in force. There are half a million demonstrators and the slogans are: 'A people's Government', 'De Gaulle resign!' 'More power for the workers!' Mendès-France declares that he is willing to undertake leadership of an interim government which includes Communists. The PCF shows no interest.

Thursday 30 May

De Gaulle, returning to Paris, declares that he has decided not to retire and cancels the referendum; he dissolves the National Assembly, announces elections for 23 and 30 June and threatens sterner, but unspecified, measures. Pompidou stays on as Prime Minister. Over 500,000 people demonstrate in favour of de Gaulle, marching from Place de la Concorde to the Arc de Triomphe. The PCF accepts the prospect of elections. The CGT re-opens negotiations. The revolutionary movements and groups reject the elections. The UNEF attempts in vain to persuade the unions to organise a common demonstration in reply to de Gaulle.

50 · An Englishman in Paris as the Crisis reached its peak

This graphic description of the Events during the final week is by Mervyn Jones, who arrived in Paris on Monday, 27 May.

The 'New Statesman', 7 June 1968

I crossed the river and plunged into the Latin Quarter. Transformation! Every café jammed, the streets dense with people, windows brightly lit. I stop every 10 yards, either to take a leaflet or buy an amateurishly printed student paper, or to drop a coin in a collection-tin for medical aid, or to listen to one of the countless impromptu discussions that attract knots of students in the roadway. Not a cop to be seen: on the Boulevard St Michel, students with armbands control the traffic, clear a path for an occasional car with *'Serrez s'il vous plaît, camarades!'* This is the republic of free Paris, the community of living ideas and exploding hopes, the *de facto* independent state which someone calls 'our revolutionary Vatican'.

Signs of battle? The stumps of sawn trees, asphalt freshly laid (a permanent improvement) where paving-stones had been torn up, a few kiosks burned out by police grenades. But seldom a single broken window, seldom a damaged building. Throughout the troubles there wasn't even a hint of looting, barely a single petty theft: student patrols were on the watch, and anyway no one thought of it. Local people laugh or reply with outraged denials to the stories of 'the underworld', of 'anarchy', disseminated in unison by the autho-

rities and the communist press. Bookshops, sandwich-bars and chemists are open late into the night.

I push my way into the Sorbonne. The vast courtyard is filled with the same endlessly talking groups. Total tolerance is the unbroken rule; Maoists offer their intellectual wares side by side with upholders of Yugoslav self-management, Trotskyists with anarchists, Zionists with advocates of Arab liberation. Victor Hugo presides benevolently, red flag strapped to his stone hand.

The young men are intense but strangely calm with a fine inner confidence; eyes red from sleepless nights, but mostly with freshly shaven cheeks or trimmed beards. The girls are lovely with their pale faces, long hair, big serious eyes, and those who aren't intrinsically beautiful are rendered beautiful by their faith and their vivacity. Love is incorporated into discussion by means of squeezed hands and rapid kisses. A pair of militant lesbians, both dazzling, embrace boldly.

Tuesday morning: I go to the École des Beaux Arts in search of the revolutionary posters that were being sold 'for the struggle', but collectors have cleaned up already. Notices on the doors announce 'Bicycle bureau'; 'Petrol for ambulances collected here'; 'Blood donors'; 'Clothes washed cleaned and lent (modern styles)'. In the university there's more

work being done than in a normal academic year. Architects are busy on the problem of building accidents due to hasty construction for the sake of profit. Sociologists are collecting evidence for a future White Book on police atrocities (I read a few statements and feel sick). Last night a conference of 1,600 people from all levels of the film industry worked out a reform plan.

I spend two hours in the occupied Odéon Theatre, *'tribune libre'* for day and night discussion. An African student is holding forth about the problems of the third world. Some impatience from those preoccupied with French events; a voice demands, *'De quelle révolution s'agit-il?'* Another voice replies: *'Du monde!'* Everyone cheers. Then a man who says he's a worker declares that he doesn't care about the underdeveloped countries. A girl gesticulates: 'But you live on them! Do you take sugar in coffee?' A building foreman urges student-worker unity, remarks that he's never been in this theatre before but he likes it. A girl answers: 'I'd never been in the Renault works till last week but I liked that too.'

Wednesday was the day of breathless hope, when de Gaulle left Paris and it seemed magically possible that he was abandoning power. The communists and the CGT staged an immense demonstration, marching from the Place de la Bastille to the heart of 'respectable' Paris. Half an hour after the first contingents moved off, others were waiting to get into the huge Place; I watched a group of youngsters dancing the Carmagnole and singing the revolutionary songs that are the Frenchman's inheritance. For the first time anyone can remember, the communist *service d'ordre* had to allow Maoist and Trotskyist groups to join in under their own banners—absolutely no discord or bad feeling about this.

On Thursday came the counter-attack. De Gaulle's broadcast caught me in the barber's chair. It didn't scare anyone—the barber remarked: 'He wants to die like a hero'—but soon there were signs of the mobilisation of Gaullist shock-troops. Cars draped in *tricolores* (and mysteriously full of petrol) raced along Boulevard St Germain blowing their horns and trying to provoke trouble. Later, I was to find the Champs Élysées blocked solid with them after midnight, all tooting the '*Algérie Française*' rhythm.

At six I went to watch the Gaullist demonstration along the Champs Élysées. Stopping in a café to make a phone call, I heard the man ahead of me say: 'Darling? I'm just going to march for a bit—bring the car to collect me at the Étoile.' The crowd was certainly huge; I don't think it was bigger than the CGT's, but beyond a certain point estimates become guesses. Almost entirely well-dressed, inclined to be elderly, people unused to this kind of action and enjoying it in the manner of American businessmen at a college reunion or an American Legion spree. Chants of '*La France au travail*', '*Nettoyez la Sorbonne*', '*C'est nous la majorité!*' The strangest thing was to see US-owned firms with *tricolores* all over their balconies and cheered by the marchers.

But the demonstration had an ugly side. The jingo, xenophobic slogan of '*La France aux Français!*'—a traditional classic of the Right—was often heard. So was another old favourite: '*La police avec nous!*' The shout which I didn't hear myself, but which was well attested enough to be reported in *Le Monde*, was '*Cohn-Bendit à Dachau!*' That night an Italian friend went to the cinema; when Cohn-Bendit appeared in the newsreel there were cries of '*Au four!*' (To the crematorium). On the march I saw plenty of faces—mostly the well-powdered faces of ladies in hats—distorted with hatred and the hunger for revenge. A contingent of nuns was yelling 'Mitterrand in prison!' Setting the picture beside that of the day before, I saw the eternal '*deux Frances*'—sansculottes and aristos, Commune and Versailles. The enemy is still Shelley's: 'old Custom, legal Crime, and bloody Faith'.

Back to the Sorbonne late in the evening. A student was speaking through a loudhailer: 'It's the time of double power. Organise your action committees everywhere, organise the power of the workers by hand and brain!' But nobody was organising. The two great boulevards of the Quarter were thicker than ever before with chattering groups; our Speakers' Corner multiplied by fifty, except that there were no speakers and listeners, only the immense harmony of the endless discussion. One never had a sense of defeat, but one did have a sense of unreality as the vital hours trickled away. There were people enough—and to spare—to set up a rival government, to take and garrison a stronghold like the Hotel de Ville. But the hard logic remains: you don't make a revolution without leadership, without a revolutionary party. The party didn't want revolution, those who wanted revolution had no party. Simple.

51 · Students talk to the people

'Le Monde',
29 May 1968
When the 'Hotheads' go to the people

About fifteen students from Nanterre have chosen the square of Batignolles to go to the people, to 'their' people: note that these young lads and girls live in this district of the 17th arondissement which is part of the catchment area for the Faculty of Letters of Nanterre. It was one of the district meetings that the militants of the Mouvement du 22 mars held in Paris on Monday.

While the mums were quietly watching their children in this large park, near the railings overlooking the railway which leads from the Gare St Lazare, a curious crowd of about sixty was listening to the 'hotheads'. It was a mixed public reflecting this district which is on the frontier between an average middle-class area and workers' tenements; clerks, technicians, a few students and some workmen of all ages, some of whom had just been at a brief meeting organised in the same place, at 5 o'clock, by the CGT.

A militant of the Mouvement du 22 mars said that they thought the policy of UNEF was adventurist. 'We must avoid all bloody confrontations,' they declared. 'It is suicide to want to go on like the UNEF organising mass demonstrations after the Government's warning against all gatherings. We consider that there are better things to do from now on: we should have more meetings in the Quartier in order to explain the meaning of the referendum.'

The audience listened with total interest to the explanations and particularly to what they said about the Communist Party and the CGT.

'We asked to be allowed to speak at the CGT meeting which has just finished. We were refused the microphone. Ever since our movement started, we have had insults and beatings up from the militants of the Communist party.'

'The CGT and the Communist Party are tools of the Government,' shouted a young worker.

'But your Cohn-Bendit', says another 'has said that the French are amorphous. That's not true.'

'It was a mistake,' confessed a 'hothead'.

Despite the drizzle which was beginning to fall, the discussions in small groups continued for more than two hours. Just as in the Sorbonne people were talking about everything. It reminded you of the Sunday meetings in Hyde Park.

'The point is,' declared a student from Nanterre emphatically, 'to paralyse the country without shedding blood.' This prospect of paralysis did not seem to make the audience very enthusiastic. 'Where is it going to get you? What is your recipe for society?'—'I am not a cook, I haven't got any recipes,' replied a 'hothead'.

The exchanges continued beneath the trees.

'We could certainly do without a lot of things', said one petit-bourgeois, 'for example the treble chance is stupid'—'What,' replied another, 'everybody should be free to amuse himself as he likes.'

Some were saying that there were too many students and that they would be less wasteful about their future if there was some form of selection. 'There's all

sorts at Nanterre', a workman was saying. 'I understood that I hadn't got any basis for further education and I went to work. There are students who would do well to do the same.'

The little groups came together again to watch a confrontation between the 'hotheads' and the student who was a member of the Communist Party who had bravely appeared. 'We have to unite all those who are fed-up with Gaullism', he said.

'Is that how you think of building Socialism?', a militant of the Mouvement du 22 mars replied.

'The Communist Party wants to instal a real democracy,' replied the young Communist.

'That's going back to the Fourth Republic,' was what he was told.

The caretaker in charge of the square was listening impassively to these homilies about creative disorder, until a lady appeared with her dog. He at once rushed off to ensure that the prohibition was respected. On the other side of the railings, people obstinately continued their daily game of bowls.

52 · Rioters explain their motives

**'Le Monde',
29 May 1968
The criminal world of Nantes**

'Why am I demonstrating? Mainly because I am against the added value tax. . . .' An unexpected reply from the lips of a boy of 18 who, with a stone in each hand, was challenging the police on Friday, who were massed all round the Prefecture at Nantes. 'Yes, last week, I bought a silencer for my mo-ped and I had to pay 20 per cent more for it than last year,' says the boy, brushing back his

hair with his hand. He wears a leather jacket and blue jeans. 'Anyway, now, when the cops ask for my papers, they'll get my mo-ped in their mugs.'

At the corner at the Rue de Strasbourg, in front of the window of a hairdresser's, which was smashed at the moment when the Head of State was speaking, a 19-year-old boy, well-dressed, with a cudgel in his right hand and a dustbin lid in his left, gets his breath before rushing back into the thick of the fight: 'I am a worker. I am demonstrating for higher wages.

And then also about pretty well everything. I feel really mad. I hate the guts of those twerps. I have got my revenge to take. . . .' The criminal world, in fact, as M. Fouchet would say, interpreting the virtuous indignation of the middle-class? Yes, of course, if by that you mean that these boys are in revolt against a society unable to give them a job and obliged from the earliest age to rely on violence and robbery.

In Nantes, in the unbreathable atmosphere of streets drenched with tear-gas grenades, you found yourself rubbing shoulders with demonstrators from all sorts of backgrounds, temporarily brought together by a common desire for rebellion and change, expressed in an often confused manner, stimulated by the news of 'what was happening in Paris' and also by the advice of a number of 'specialists' in Molotov cocktails and tearing up cobblestones from the roads.

Why these barricades? Why 24 wounded? There is no placard there to tell you. No explanatory slogan is shouted by this crowd made up of students and workers who have not been brought there by any trade union call-to-arms. 'I'm a student. I got by. I was caught up in the milieu. If the UNEF gave us orders, we could do terrible things. Only the UNEF here is controlled by the Anarchists. So they refuse to organise demonstrations. . . .'

A young agricultural labourer, who's a bit shy. He has come back after the organisers of the peasant demonstration gave the order to disperse. Now here he is, wiping his eyes with his handkerchief and being initiated into the technique of tearing up the cobbles: 'Why am I here? Because in three hours of violence, you get more than in three years of negotiations, damn it!' This is hardly the moment to talk about the experience of the past, 'of the 1914 war,' or of '1936': 'The old, they're the ones! It's all their fault that we're in this mess!'

A bearded boy with a helmet who has been wandering round all night with a club in one hand and a cobblestone in the other: 'I'm a worker, but I'm wholeheartedly with the Mouvement du 22 mars. Have I got any political commitment? Let's say that I'm a socialist in the broadest sense of the term. More an anarchist! . . .' Another figure that stands out from this 'long hot night', is the worker who, armed with a navvy's shovel found in a building-site, has spent his time systematically smashing, without apparent rage, all the window-panes on the ground-floor of the new Prefecture: 'I'm a worker. I earn 550 francs a month, that's all.' A man 40-years-old, with many decorations. 'I was a professional soldier. I've seen Indo-China and Algeria. Today we've reached sticking point. When the snowball melts, there's a moment when nothing's left.' I found this man again the next day by chance in a small-holding in the countryside: he'd joined up because at 14 he was an agricultural labourer. . . .

The last word is probably the one shouted by 500 demonstrators comprising the hard core who were addressed by the CGT spokesman Andrieu about 1.30 in the morning and whom he begged to accept an interview with the Prefect. 'What you want, is to permit Cohn-Bendit to return to France?'

'To hell with that. . . .'

'Are you ready to fight for the right to strike?'

'It's all the same to us. . . .'

'Well what *do* you want, comrades? The Government's resignation?'

'Yes, yes. . . .'

A massive 'yes' which was not the one that everybody was expecting.

53 · Turmoil in public opinion

On the day of de Gaulle's second speech, dissolving the National Assembly and fixing new elections, the results of a poll were published by IFOP. Taken at the beginning of the final week of the crisis they are an interesting reflection of the turmoil induced in people's judgement by the May Events.

One-third of the population of Paris fears the present crisis will turn into revolution, civil war or anarchy, according to the French Institute of Public Opinion.

A poll taken on Monday and published today shows that only the Communist-controlled General Confederation of Labour and other unions have gone up in the people's estimation. Political parties, the National Assembly, student movements and the police have lost in popularity.

The questions asked in the poll were designed to elicit the extent to which people's views have been altered by events, rather than to assess support for political groupings.

The results reveal enormous swings in opinion. For example, while 44 per cent have a worse opinion of student movements, 38 per cent have a better one.

The Gaullist party has declined in the estimation of 42 per cent of the people interviewed. The popularity of the Communist party declined by 35 per cent and the Federation of the Left's following declined by 29 per cent.

The National Assembly, which rejected a motion to censure the Government last week, has lost the support of 37 per cent of those interviewed.

The internal crisis should result in financial advantages to workers in the opinion of 38 per cent and the same percentage believed that these advantages could be gained without an economic crisis. However, 48 per cent consider an economic disturbance unavoidable.

54 · Gaullist alarmism

Statement of the Minister of the Interior, M. Christian Fouchet 27 May 1968

Once more Paris has been through a night of rioting.

There is a first element. The students have been carried away by their excitement, even though the university reform which they demand is going to be carried out.

The second element is from the criminal world, which is daily more numerous. It is against this latter that the police, even now, is fighting. This criminal element which is emerging from the underworld of Paris and which is really desperate, hiding behind the students, is fighting with a murderous rage. It is the task of the Government to put an end to the action of this criminal element as soon as possible.

The third element are the Anarchists, who are certainly very well organised for street warfare, for guerilla fighting.

The police have to fight against these well-armed people who are using catapults and even iron bars. This cannot go on for ever. Parisians should know the dirty side of what is going on. I ask that Paris should spew up this criminal element which dishonours it.

55 · Gaullist leaflet

A leaflet issued by the Gaullist CDR in an attempt to rally the Right-wing students to their side

Students . . .
On 11 November 1940 your elders were demonstrating at the Arc de Triomphe and were being shot by the Germans.
In 1968, foreign agitators are insulting France.

> 'The French flag is made to be
> torn up and turned into a
> red flag. . . .'
>   Cohn-Bendit, Amsterdam, 22 May.

That's not what you are fighting for. Show that it isn't!
Join the CDR Youth section.

56 · PCF Warning against the Left

Warning   The Communist Party renews its warning against demonstrations decided outside the organisations of the working-class.

In order to defeat all new provocations which could gravely prejudice the great movement now taking place for the demands of the workers and for a government of the people of democratic unity, it appeals to people not to take part in the demonstrations organised for today Monday 27 May by the UNEF.

57 · Mitterrand's Press conference 28 May 1968

Mitterrand makes his bid for power, proposing a provisional government headed by Mendès-France or himself.

... our country does not have to choose between anarchy and the man of whom I shall not speak today except to say that he can no longer make history. The task is to lay the basis for a democratic socialism and to open to youth the exalting perspective of the new alliance of socialism and liberty.

... It does not matter who is the man that undertakes this task initially. What matters is that it is accomplished.

... For the moment I would like to make the following points in the great debate in which the French are now engaged:

1   Republicans will naturally say No to the referendum-plebiscite. But as the referendum is only a subterfuge, it is necessary at once to take account of the power vacuum and to organise the succession;

2   The departure of General de Gaulle after the 16 June, if not before, will naturally bring about the disappearance of the Prime Minister and of his government;

In this hypothesis I propose that a provisional caretaker government be set up at once. Its task will be threefold: to get the state machine moving again by being prepared to listen to the many groupings of workers and students who are ardently and unselfishly working out the indispensable reforms of our economic, social and university system; to satisfy the just demands of the various social and professional groups; and organise the practical conditions for a presidential election. It will stay in office until the election of a new president of the Republic, to take place during July. It will consist of 10 members chosen without undue exclusiveness or outdated political bias, as was the case in 1944 in different yet comparable conditions.

3   One of the first acts of the President of the Republic will be to dissolve the National Assembly.... The Assembly will be renewed in October.... The citizens will then decide freely.... This aim could not be achieved if provocation and repression are able to profit from disorder. Those who, rightly, do not accept the established order, must find in cohesion and discipline the real means to make certain of their victory.

But naturally two questions will spring to mind at once:

'Who will form the provisional government?' If necessary, I will assume this responsibility. But others may have a legitimate claim. I think first of M. Pierre Mendès-France. In any case, I repeat, it is not a problem of men but a political choice.

'And who will be the President of the Republic?' A free vote will decide. But I hereby announce, since the possible date is only 18 days away, that I am a candidate.

58 · The response of the Centre

The following day, Senator Jean Lecanuet, chairman of the Centre Démocrate, staked his own claim in the new arrangements foreseen by Mitterrand.

There is only one way to save France: to give the country a new government urgently—a government of public safety.
... We must reconcile all men of progress. If M. Mendès-France agrees, if he is ready to protect freedom, if he has a European and social policy, it only remains to discuss the men he will choose, whom he will consider most suitable to undertake this heavy task.

59 · The PCF's response to Mitterrand

Statement by Waldeck Rochet, Secretary 28 May 1968

There can be in France no Left policy and no social progress without the active participation of the Communists, all the more so it is not serious to claim to be moving towards Socialism without Communism and even less while practising anti-Communism as at the Charléty stadium.

Of course, the Communist Party says No to the Gaullist referendum. On the other hand, with millions of workers engaged in struggle, we do not intend to see the present régime substituted by another régime which would not satisfy the demands of the workers on the pretext that they were no longer valid and which would mark a return to a detestable past, characterised by the fact that governments claiming to be of the Left practised policies of the Right while keeping the working-class and the Communist Party away from any share in the government of the country.

Nor do we intend to prepare the way for a régime subservient to American policies.

60 · The Gaullist response to Mitterrand

Statement by Robert Poujade 29 May 1968

Even if one accepts the risky hypothesis of M. Mitterrand, if, that is, contrary to all expectation, a majority should reject the reforms which the country is awaiting, M. Mitterrand could not take power except by violating the legality of the Republic.

In fact, should there be a vacancy of the Presidency of the Republic, the constitutional dispositions concerning the interim do not authorise either the President of the Senate or of the Assembly to dismiss the Government. The so-called 'provisional government' of M. Mitterrand could not therefore be the result of anything but a coup d'état.

61 · The turn of the tide: de Gaulle's radio broadcast. 16.30, 30 May 1968

Frenchwomen, Frenchmen, as the trustee of national and republican legitimacy, I have, for the past twenty-four hours, considered every possibility, without exception, which would enable me to preserve that legitimacy. I have made my resolutions. In the present circumstances I shall not resign. I have a mandate from the people. I shall fulfil it. I shall not dismiss the Prime Minister, whose value, solidity and ability deserve admiration from all. He will propose to me the changes which he thinks useful in the composition of the Government. I am dissolving the National Assembly today. I proposed to the country a referendum, which would give every citizen a chance to prescribe a profound reform of our economy and our university, and at the same time to say whether or not they still had confidence in me by the only acceptable way, the way of democracy.

I find that the present situation materially prevents this referendum from taking place. That is why I am postponing it. As for the general election, it will be held within the time limit laid down by the constitution—unless it is intended to gag the entire French people, by preventing them from expressing themselves at the same time as they are prevented from living, and with the same methods which are used to prevent the students from studying, the teachers from teaching, and the workers from working. These methods are intimidation, intoxication and tyranny exercised by groups long organised for that purpose, and by a party which is a totalitarian enterprise even if it already has rivals in that respect.

If therefore this situation of force continues I shall have, in order to preserve the Republic, to adopt, in accordance with the constitution, other methods than an immediate vote of the country. In any case, civic action must be organised everywhere and at once. This must be done to help the Government in the first place, and then locally, to help the Prefects, who will assume or reassume the role of commissioners of the Republic, in their task which is to ensure as far as possible the livelihood of the population and to prevent subversion at every moment and in every place.

France is indeed threatened with dictatorship. People are trying to compel her to resign herself to a power which would impose itself in the midst of national despair. This power would then be essentially that of the conqueror, that is to say, the power of totalitarian communism.

Naturally, it would to start with be coloured with a deceptive appearance by using the ambition and hatred of discarded politicians. Later, these persons would carry no more than their own weight, which would not be much. I say no, the Republic will not abdicate, the people will come to their senses. Progress, independence and peace will win the day together with freedom. Long live the Republic! Long live France!

62 · The PCF reaction to de Gaulle's announcement of elections.

Speech by Waldeck Rochet, Secretary (extract) 30 May 1968

We have said it and we repeat it, we believe that the Gaullist régime has had its day. It no longer corresponds to the needs of the moment. We must defeat it at the coming national elections at which our Communist Party will take an active part with its candidates and its programme. What the masses of the French people really want today is not just changes of a minister or two, it is a complete change of policy and of régime.

The Communists are in fact on every occasion responsible men acting with lucidity and coolness, attentive that each of their decisions, each of their acts, should be of real service to the interests of the workers, of the people and of the country.

On the other hand, the pseudo-revolutionaries who call themselves Anarchists, Maoists or Trotskyists are performing objectively the greatest service to the Gaullist régime, for, by their methods and their anti-Communism, they are aiming to divide the working-class, to give a bad name to the revolutionary movement and to democracy and by the same token to deprive the workers of their natural allies. They are playing the game of the Gaullist régime.

63 · Press comment

a) 'Le Figaro', 31 May 1968 (leading article)

Why weren't these words spoken earlier?

Would we have reached the point we did if the Chief of State, giving up his trip to Rumania, had then spoken with as much vigour and energy as yesterday evening?

A confrontation ought to be avoided, since it is only the people in the last resort and in the wishes of all republicans who will have in the days to come the task of making a sovereign decision.

Between the Tricolore and the banners with funereal colours, Paris has chosen. France too.

b) 'La Nation' (leading article)

Each day which passes thrusts the dagger a little further into the body of France. Each day which passes wounds equally, without their realising, those Frenchmen who are poorest, those who are always dependent on their work, that is to say on the economic activity of the country. The trade unions know it. The politicians too. They have deliberately aimed the dagger themselves in the direction which they thought would be decisive: the direction of the heart. The power which they claim would be a power usurped.

c) 'Le Combat' (quote from leading article)

De Gaulle is playing off the population against the People, he is drumming up the Fascists disguised as committees of support, he is making certain that the military are behind him, he is arousing panic in order to be restored to power.

The appeal to insurrection, when the latter is the bearer of the future, is a sacred duty. The provocation of a People is always a crime.

Who claims to defend de Gaulle? The workers? They are all on strike against him. The youths? They have risked their lives against his régime. Children? They are rebelling in their high schools and in their primary schools against the established order. There are only the others left, those who keep silent because they have nothing to say when the People is in danger, because they are afraid, those who do not count when it is a question of defending progress.

d) 'Le Monde', 1 June 1968

It is perfectly pointless to regret that de Gaulle the man, however exceptional he may be, cannot be what one would like him to be. All the same, for the most part, the decisions taken are those which had to be taken and which should have been taken earlier. A dangerous confrontation is now in progress. It is up to the trade unionists and the Communists to convince themselves that there is no point in aggravating the misfortunes of the public which could easily be blamed on them. It is up to the Gaullists who have now become thoroughly cocky not to forget that liberty can be killed when one believes that one is defending it and that certain forms of 'civic action' soon begin to rhyme with Fascist reaction.

On 31 May, commenting upon de Gaulle's speech of the day before, the International Herald Tribune still sees the prospect for the General in pessimistic terms.

'The International Herald Tribune', 31 May 1968

To a world braced for the state of flux which a resignation by President de Gaulle would mean for France, the new confrontation signalled by his radio address came as a shock. The democratic logic of the President's radio address was impeccable.

But tempers have risen; the workers and students have tasted power; respect for forms of government has been vitiated. Now the broad hint of mobilizing groups for 'civic action' against disorders, and of relying on the President's extraordinary powers to end national chaos, threatens nothing less than civil war.

Charles de Gaulle has ridden out many storms and directed many whirlwinds since he first addressed his countrymen from London nearly 28 years ago. But then he was a vigorous two-star general, defying an aging, tired group of defeatists. Now the gale has been whipped up by the young, and de Gaulle represents another generation, another war, another cast of thought. The forecast must be for the roughest of weather.

Commenting upon de Gaulle's speech of 30 May, The Daily Telegraph looks ahead not without a trace of satisfaction, at the economic price of the May Events.

The 'Daily Telegraph', 31 May 1968

What chance is there that this opposition, both political and social, will now be deflected into constitutional paths? The prospects of the immediate crisis easing, of the trade unionists returning to work and the students to their desks, are probably good. Many Frenchmen will wish to rally to the Government, as they have often done in the past and as the President clearly expects now, in the name of order—for the time being. And the crumbling political situation has been neutralised by the dissolution of the National Assembly.

Meanwhile, the strikers will have to be bought off with large wage increases, and those famous gold reserves, not to mention Gaullist military and diplomatic designs abroad, will take a nasty knock. The ominous pressure on the franc this week is a timely reminder of just how difficult the coming months will be for France, with or eventually without President de Gaulle.

Sequel

8 · Aftermath

Chronology of the Crisis (31 May—30 June)

Friday 31 May

The unions continue their negotations with the Government and the employers, industry by industry. Some workers go back to work. The police drive away the strike pickets from post offices. The public transport workers reach an agreement, but in general the strike continues. Pompidou presents his caretaker Government which contains some left-wing Gaullists, including René Capitant.

Saturday 1 June

The UNEF organises a demonstration in Paris together with the Mouvement du 22 mars, the CAL, and the FO. 30,000 people march from Montparnasse to the Gare d'Austerlitz. Cohn-Bendit is at the head of the procession. After the demonstration the students move to the Renault and Citroën factories which are still occupied by the workers. The CGT criticises the demonstration, defining it as untimely. In the provinces there are Gaullist demonstrations. Petrol is made available for the Whitsun holiday and there is a mass exodus from Paris. (68 road deaths in one weekend.)

Sunday 2 June

The negotiations between the unions and their own workers become difficult in the transport and steel sectors. Strikers re-occupy the stations at Strasbourg and Mulhouse.

Monday 3 June

The steel workers' strike continues. The ORTF trade union breaks off all relations with the Ministry of Information, in protest against the failure to revise the charter of the broadcasting services, and the Director of the radio services, de Boisdeffre, and the Director of television services, Pierre Viasini, resign. Army technicians are sent in to maintain broadcasting. Twenty-three blacklegs demand the sacking of some of the strikers. The trade unions obtain a partial resumption of work in the public transport sector, on the railways, in the banks and mines.

Tuesday 4 June

Police occupy the ORTF. Negotiations with the transport authorities and the railway authorities continue. In Paris there is no public transport for fifteen hours.

Wednesday 5 June

The PCF publishes in *L'Humanité* the criticisms of Communist intellectuals who do not approve the party line on the student movement. End of the strikes in the electricity, gas, and mining sectors. The teachers obtain important concessions from the Ministry of Education.

Thursday 6 June

L'Humanité hails the end of the strikes: 'Workers in public transport, railwaymen, miners, resume work after the victory of unity. Demands dating back for several years have finally been satisfied'. At Flins, the Renault factories are occupied by thousands of CRS.

Friday 7 June

De Gaulle, interviewed on TV by the journalist Michel Droit speaks of 'participation'. He attacks the PCF but declares himself not hostile to the demands of workers and students. Meanwhile the strikes go on. The CGT denounces the intervention of 'militarily organised gangs', at Flins. The students meet at Flins with the intention of reinforcing the strike pickets of the workers in the streets around the factories. The police intervene. In Paris the students preparing to go to Flins, finding the Gare St Lazare surrounded by hundreds of CRS preventing them from entering, organise a protest demonstration. The CGT disapproves of the students' intervention, accusing them of being provocateurs working for the Government and the employers.

Saturday 8 June

The police offensive against the workers and students continues at Flins. All the roads leading to Flins are blocked by the police and several motorists not involved in the troubles are arrested and their cars damaged. Tear-gas grenades are thrown at the demonstrators and into houses. The strikes go on. In the steel industry the negotiations between unions and workers are broken off.

Sunday 9 June

Georges Bidault, the former leader of the OAS, returns to France from Belgium. The police take action against foreigners, particularly students, who are arrested and expelled from the country. The balance-sheet of the clashes of Friday and Saturday at Flins is 60 wounded and 240 arrested.

Monday 10 June

Election campaign begins. On Monday morning the whole region around Flins is surrounded by police. Some workers arrive for work at 5.25. On the bridge at Meulan some students stop them to say that the strike is continuing. The police charge, bombs are thrown, arrests take place. A high school student drowns in the Seine after being charged violently by the CRS.

At Sochaux workers of the Peugeot factory are collected by buses during the night and taken to the factory. In the morning some young workers down tools and persuade their workmates to start the strike again. At 3 pm, ten thousand workers vote for a strike and to occupy the factory. During the night the CRS climb the boundary wall and attack the strikers. In Paris the students demonstrate in the Quartier Latin during the evening to protest against the police violence against the workers.

Tuesday 11 June

At Sochaux the battle flares up again. At 10 am the workers enter the factory armed with stones. A twenty-four year old worker is shot by the CRS. Another eleven people are wounded by fire-arms. Another worker, choked by tear-gas falls from a wall on which he had climbed to get away from the CRS and dies of a fracture of the skull. Two other workers are seriously wounded. Peugeot and the Government yield: the factory remains closed. The CRS are withdrawn. The UNEF and the other student organisations call a protest demonstration against the killings. In the afternoon the police arrest numerous high school students and surround the Gare de l'Est, the starting point for the demonstration. The demonstrators then move towards the Quartier Latin and clash with the police in front of the

Faculty of Medicine. In the Quartier Latin, barricades go up once more. The clashes go on throughout the night and the students take refuge in the Sorbonne which is at once besieged by the police who throw tear-gas grenades through the windows. 2,000 arrests are made (44 receive jail sentences, 114 foreigners are expelled from the country), 75 barricades are built and torn down. The total of wounded is thought to be over 1,000.

Wednesday 12 June   The Government prohibits all demonstrations until the day of the elections (23 June), and dissolves extreme left groups: the FER, the JCR, the Voix Ouvrière, the Mouvement du 22 mars, the UJCM-L, (but neither the UEC nor the right-wing Occident group).

Thursday 13 June   More left-wing organisations declared outlaw: the PCI and PCM-LF. Arrests of many members of the dissolved organisations are carried out. The only protest comes from Guy Mollet.

Saturday 15 June   Salan and Lacheroy, two of the most important members of the OAS, are released from prison together with ex-colonel Argoud and seven others: no member of the OAS is now held in prison.

Sunday 16 June   Using a pretext to gain entry, the police reoccupy the Sorbonne, which is to remain closed until further notice.

Tuesday 18 June   The strike still continues, and is carried on by several hundred thousand workers for some days longer. In the Renault factories resumption of work takes place despite the fact that many workers are opposed to it. At Flins resumption is possible thanks to the large number of workers abstaining from the vote.

Thursday 20 June   Peugeot and Berliet strikers go back to work.

Sunday 23 June   General election: first ballot shows considerable gains by the Gaullists. Disunity of the Left continues to grow.

Tuesday 25 June   Citroën strikers go back to work.

Sunday 30 June   General election: second ballot. The PCF and FGDS lose over 10 per cent of their votes compared with 1967, the Centre (PDM) loses over 30 per cent, while the Gaullists (UDR) gaining almost 20 per cent, are returned to power with a 'chambre introuvable'.

64 · The last days of the Student Soviet

How the student occupation of the Sorbonne ended.

The last days of the Student Soviet were as sad as the first had been heroic. For greater efficiency, perhaps for greater security, the hard-core leaders moved out of the Sorbonne, abandoning it to its fairground role. A group of 'International Situationists'—a latterday incarnation of surrealism—seized the university loudspeaker system for a time and issued extravagant directives. Worse still, the halls and corridors grew filthy with the shuffling of a thousand feet. Here too, tramps moved in, and beatniks, and people who had nowhere else to sleep. Rats moved up from the sewers; police spies came through the front door. Some youngsters took hash and needed daily treatment. The infirmary became a scandal. About thirty thugs, petty criminals, ex-Foreign Legionaires, deserters—calling themselves 'the *Katangais*'—moved into a Sorbonne basement and spread uncertain terror about them. They too, in their way hated society, and had come to help the students, but they brought disrepute. They had a couple of small-bore sports rifles, some ugly looking knives, a few sticks and bars, some lengths of chain, and a painted girl or two. One night in mid-June there was a scuffle, and they were thrown out by a students' *service d'ordre*, mobilized by the occupation committee.

The committee also called for mops and water and disinfectant, to give the vast building a spring-clean. But it never finished the job. At 2 am on Sunday, 16 June, a young man was dumped at the Sorbonne infirmary with a knife wound. The students immediately took him off to hospital; but a police inquiry followed. Seizing on this pretext, the government sent in a force of police which met little resistance. The last teachers and students were driven out singing the *Internationale*. Small-scale skirmishing broke out on the boulevards. A few stones were thrown, a few gas grenades. But the student riposte had no sting to it. The red and black flags were hauled down from the Sorbonne and replaced by the Tricolor. One colourful phase of student action was at an end.

65 · The last stands: Flins and Sochaux

A few hours before General de Gaulle's television interview this evening the first big clash of the French strike movement occurred between workers and riot police at the Renault plant at Flins, some 40 miles West of Paris.

The workers, supported by a number of students, were trying to resume control of the plant from which the police had expelled strike pickets early yesterday. About 10 people were injured.

The trouble began this morning when several thousand workers and about 200 students who had slipped through the police road-blocks, held a meeting in a square about 600 yards from the works.

After demanding a resumption of negotiations with the management and the removal of police from the works, the demonstrators began marching towards the works. They came up against a strong force of mobile gendarmes.

About 2,000 riot police were stationed around the works and a similar number were held in the area in reserve.

It is not clear who made the first attack. But the demonstrators apparently tried to push through the iron railings set up by the police to keep the approaches to the works clear and were repulsed with a barrage of tear-gas bombs.

They counter-attacked with fire-bombs, bolts and nuts, paving stones and anything that came to hand. The police then charged with new barrages of tear-gas.

This afternoon the riot squads were pursuing demonstrators across the countryside about a mile and a half from the works.

Many shop windows appear to have been broken in the fighting and the streets of the village of Elizabethville, where the demonstrators met, were littered with debris.

Demonstrators and riot police clashed again at the Peugeot car factory at Sochaux in south-east France after a lunch-time truce. Groups of young men repeatedly harrassed the police cordon around the factory, hurling stones and other missiles, and the police replied with tear-gas and baton charges.

More serious still, for its repercussions on the labour situation, was the death of a young worker at the Sochaux plant and the wounding of another by a bullet. This has produced a wave of indignation among unions and workers alike.

The left-wing students' organisation, UNEF, has interpreted the drowning of the youth at Flins as an act of assassination by the police. Last night to avenge his death 1,000 students attacked the police in the Quartier Latin besieging two police stations, hurling petrol bombs, building 9 barricades and setting fire to a number of cars. Election placards provided ready and suitably symbolic fuel for bonfires. The police retaliated by clearing the streets by means of the now customary tear-gas grenades and bulldozer technique. Fighting went on until 7 am today.

66 · Communist dissenters

Extract from a letter addressed by a group of Communist intellectuals to the leadership of the PCF 26 May 1968

Fifty thousand demonstrators were shouting, at the Gare de Lyons, their anger against the Government decision which violated the amnesty by forbidding Cohn-Bendit to return to French territory. Many Communists were there but the Party was not.

Thus the provocations of the Government were facilitated and it was helped in its desire to isolate and crush the student movement. Yet without this movement to catalyse the will of the masses to engage in the struggle, the factories would never have been occupied, the Minimum National Guaranteed Wage would never have been raised and other prospects would never have been opened before the struggling working-class whose role is decisive.

The gap between the Communists and the mass of students and intellectuals might have the most tragic consequences. A dialogue must be established as soon as possible. The debate that these events is imposing on the directions, the structure and the future of the revolutionary movement cannot now be avoided. A frank analysis of reality, of the value of bold political initiatives must permit us to set up links with the new forces which have been revealed in the struggle for socialism and liberty.

67 · PCF view of Flins

'L'Humanité', 8 June 1968

An End to Provocations
While the workers in the engineering industry are conducting with discipline and resolution a strike that both the employers and the Government together are forcing them to prolong, serious incidents have occurred at the Renault factory at Flins.

The occupation of the Flins factory by the CRS had not affected the determination of the strikers. Under the lying excuse of 'helping the workers', commandos led by Alain Geismar have openly provoked clashes, thus providing the Gaullist police with the opportunity of intervening.

These Geismar commandos, though they have nothing to do with the struggle for university demands, are militarily organised and have now gone over to provocation against the working-class movement.

They help Gaullism at a moment when the latter is resisting desperately the demands of the engineering workers. At Flins and elsewhere they have made themselves the accomplices of the Renault management and of the Government, the accomplices of the bosses of the engineering industry at the very moment when the latter has broken off negotiations with the trade unions.

These adventurers have attempted to derail the great student movement for a democratic university, they have denied the economic nature of the working-class struggle and have sought to drag the workers and the students into adventures. They give the Government new ways of blackmailing the country towards a civil war on the eve of the elections.

68 · General Election results

	1968	%	%		1967	%	%
Registered electors	28,171,635		100·	Registered electors	28,291,838		100·
Abstentions	5,631,892		19·99	Abstentions	5,404,687		19·10
Votes cast	22,539,743		80·	Votes cast	22,887,151		80·89
Spoilt papers	401,086		1·42	Spoilt papers	494,834		1·74
Net number of votes	22,138,657	100		Net number of votes	22,392,317	100	
Communists	4,435,357	20.03		Communists	5,029,808	22·46	
PSU	874,212	3·94		PSU	506,592	2·26	
FGDS	3,654,003	16·50		FGDS	4,207,166	18·79	
Other left-wing parties	133,100	0·60		Centre parties	3,017,447	13·47	
PDM	2,290,165	10·34		Other moderates	878,472	3·92	
Other moderates	410,699	1·85		Gaullists	8,558,056	38·22	
UDR, Independent Republicans and other Gaullists	10,201,024	46·05		Others, including extreme right	194,776	0·87	
Others, including extreme right	140,097	0·63					

COMPARISON

Difference in votes cast	− 253,317	
Communists	− 594,451	− 2·43
PSU	+ 367,620	+ 1·68
FGDS, etc.	− 420,063	− 1·69
PDM, etc.	− 1,195,055	− 5·20
UDR, Independent Republicans and other Gaullists	+ 1,642,968	+ 7·83
Others, including extreme right	− 54,679	− 0·24

69 · Press comment on the aftermath

a) 'L'Humanité', 24 June 1968

The extravagances, the provocations, the pointless violence (although deliberately exaggerated out of all proportion by Government propaganda) of the Leftist groups, of which certain elements were manipulated by the Ministry of the Interior, have had the result that one could foresee. Historians will find it interesting to discover exactly who took the initiative of the 'barricades', of the Rue Gay-Lussac, even if the students were involved in good faith in the police trap. Each barricade, each car that was set alight brought tens of thousands of votes to the Gaullist Party, that is the truth.

b) 'Le Combat', 24 June 1968

M. Pompidou has won.... But the movement of May has not lost.... The victory of the majority is not that of France. Contrary to what the Gaullists claim, the same people will conduct the same policies with the same methods. The country did not by its vote approve Gaullist policy; it simply condemned violence. The causes of the movement of May remain intact.

c) 'Le Monde', 2 July 1968

Despite disappointments and rancour, a way forward may thus have been opened ... not without risks, for it is as difficult to dominate a great victory as to weather a defeat and to keep that respect, that consideration for others which is the foundation of true liberties.

Besides it is not just France. Almost everywhere in the world there are mysterious and painful stirrings going on. Man is so made that neither cars nor transistors, neither computers nor gadgets are sufficient in themselves to give him a reason for living, a reason which he is constrained, when his gods are dead, to look for so desperately. Perhaps the attractions of revolution and of war are only renounced by those who have already suffered too cruelly from them.

d) 'Le Nouvel Observateur', 3 July 1968

One can't blame the voters. The Party machines and the official Left never give the impression of being able to provide an efficient Government and cooperate on a new common programme. The elections were not lost on 23 nor on 30 June. They were lost on 29 May. The experts in crowd psychology claim that perhaps there was on 30 May one barricade too many, one car too many burned and that public opinion, mysteriously sensitive to imperceptible excesses, began to waver. It is doubtful. The game was lost, in fact, on 29 May, when the Left showed that it was unable to take over power. Let us remember: De Gaulle was no longer at the Elysée. Pompidou was silent. The army was looking for a political leader. The police was divided. In all the big towns, the factories and the universities shared between them the only real power in existence. The heads of the civil service were complaining that all the machinery of the State was more or less at a standstill. It was a situation which had been entirely, completely, totally brought about by Gaullism. At that moment public opinion was a thousand times more afraid of a vacuum than of disorder: how hard everyone is trying to make us forget this today! The ruling class, the employers themselves saw the maintenance in power of General de Gaulle as being a factor likely to cause civil war. These historical truths must be repeated tirelessly. On 29 May public opinion was almost unanimously turning towards the Left. The power vacuum was becoming unbearable for everybody. All the voters who in these last few days have reproached certain important people on the Left of having tried to take power illegally were then on the contrary indignant about their keeping silent. About their inaction, about their divisions. *The Left did not lose the elections because it tried to take power. It lost them because it did not take it.*

Comment from abroad on the results of the second ballot

e) 'The New York Times', 1 July 1968

Complete power means complete responsibility, as Premier Pompidou recognised in his post-election statement, which predicted a 'difficult future.' The economic difficulties the country faces will not be easy to resolve. Inflation, already under way, could wipe out the recent wage increases by winter and bring a renewal of major strikes. Resumption of the student rebellion is expected in the fall. Flight of capital has already reduced monetary reserves by well over $1 billion, and the outlook for the franc is perilous.

But the upheaval in May was not set off by economic pressures. It essentially was a revolt against the Gaullist régime, its authoritarianism and its concern with prestige abroad instead of problems at home. President de Gaulle's promise of basic reforms may point toward some solutions. But it is certain, in any event, to change the character of the régime. A turn inward by Gaullist France appears unavoidable.

f) 'The Times', 2 July 1968

The Government's immediate concern, of course, is the economy. Wages went up 13 per cent as a result of the strike settlements, and although optimistic economists suggest that French industry will be able to absorb it there are plenty of pessimists, and in any case it is perfectly clear that the weaker sectors of French industry will be hit hard. There is already high unemployment in France, and there is now a grave danger that it could rise sharply as the more efficient industries cut back on manpower and the less efficient close their doors. At the same time prices will go up even faster than usual; indeed the general rise has already begun.

Normally a strong right-wing Government, particularly one in which financial orthodoxy is as much a dogma as it is in France today, would exert every effort to keep wages down and to protect the balance of payments at the expense of the wage-earners' standard of living. The French Government has moved sharply to the right, has just won a huge majority, but it cannot employ the classical remedies. The country would not stand for it: the events of last May showed that the French working classes will not put up with the sort of burdens the British working classes have shouldered. In parliamentary terms the Government has been much strengthened by recent events. In most other respects its credibility has been very seriously damaged, and with it its ability to command events.

9 · Summing up of the May Events

70 · The historian:

One of the clearest and most acute analyses of the May Events was written by the historian Eric Hobsbawm.

There were, it is clear, two stages in the mobilisation of the revolutionary forces, both totally unexpected by the government, the official power structure and the official opposition, even by the unofficial but recognised opposition of the important left-wing literary intellectuals in Paris. (The established left-wing intelligentsia played no significant part in the May Events; Jean-Paul Sartre, with great tact and intuition, recognised this by effacing himself before Daniel Cohn-Bendit, to whom he acted merely as interviewer.) The first stage, roughly between 3 and 11 May mobilised the students. Thanks to the government's inattention, complacency, and stupidity, a movement of activists in a suburban campus was transformed into a mass movement of virtually all students in Paris, enjoying vast public support—at this stage 61 per cent of Parisians were pro-student and only 16 per cent definitely hostile—and then into a sort of symbolic insurrection of the Latin Quarter. The government retreated before it, and in so doing spread the movement to the provinces and, especially, to the workers.

The second phase of mobilisaton, from May 14 to May 27, consisted essentially in the extension of a spontaneous general strike, the largest in the history of France or perhaps of any other country, and culminated with the rejection by the strikers of the deal negotiated on their behalf between the official union leaders and the government. Throughout this period, up to May 29, the popular movement held the initiative; the government, caught on the wrong foot at the start, was unable to recover itself, and grew progressively demoralised. The same is true of conservative and moderate opinion, which was at this time passive, even paralysed. The situation changed rapidly when de Gaulle at last took action on 29 May.

The first thing to observe is that only the second phase created revolutionary possibilities (or, to put it another way, it created the need for the government to take counter-revolutionary action). The student movement by itself was a nuisance, but not a political danger. The authorities grossly underrated it, but this was largely because they were thinking about other things, including other university problems and the bureaucratic infighting between various government departments, which seemed to them more important. Yet, paradoxically, the very lack of importance of the student movement made it a most effective detonator of the workers' mobilization. Having underestimated and neglected it, the government tried to disperse it by force. When the students refused to go home, the only choice was between shooting and a public, humiliating retreat. But how could they have chosen to shoot?

Massacre is one of the last resorts of the government in stable industrial societies, since (unless directed against outsiders of one kind or another) it destroys the impression of popular consent on which they rest.

Once the velvet glove has been put on the iron fist, it is politically very risky to take it off. Massacring students, the children of the respectable middle class, not to mention ministers, is even less attractive politically than killing workers and peasants. Just because the students were only a bunch of unarmed kids who did not put the régime at risk, the government had little choice but to retreat before them. But in doing so it created the very situation it wished to avoid. It appeared to show its impotence and gave the students a cheap victory. The Paris chief of police, an intelligent man, had more or less told his minister to avoid a bluff which virtually had to be called. That the students did not believe it to be a bluff does not change the reality of the situation.

Conversely, the workers' mobilisation did put the régime in a risky position, which is why de Gaulle was finally prepared to use the ultimate weapon, civil war, by calling on the army. This was not because insurrection was the serious object of anyone, for neither the students, who may have wanted it, nor the workers, who certainly did not, thought or acted in such political terms. It was because the progressive crumbling of government authority left a void, and because the only practicable alternative government was a popular front inevitably dominated by the Communist Party. The revolutionary students may not have considered this a particularly significant political change, and most Frenchmen would almost certainly have accepted it more or less willingly.

But the Popular Front was *not* ready to occupy the vacuum left by the disintegration of Gaullism. The non-communists in the alliance dragged their feet, since the crisis demonstrated that they represented nobody except a few politicians, while the Communist Party, through its control of the strongest union federation, was for the time being the only civilian force of real significance, and would therefore have inevitably dominated the new government. The crisis eliminated the sham politics of electoral calculation and left visible only the real politics of power. But the Communists in turn had no means of forcing the date of their shotgun wedding with the other opposition groups. For they had themselves been playing the electoral game. They had not mobilized the masses whose action pushed them to the verge of power, and they had not thought of using that action to force their allies' hand. On the contrary, if Philippe Alexandre is to be believed, they seem to have regarded the strike as something that might stop them from concentrating on the really important job of keeping their allies in line.

De Gaulle, a notoriously brilliant politician, recognised both the moment when his opponents lost their momentum, and the chance of regaining his own initiative. With an apparently imminent communist-led popular front, a conservative régime could at last play out its trump card: the fear of revolution. It was, tactically speaking, a beautifully judged performance. De Gaulle did not even have to shoot. Indeed, not the least curious aspect of the entire May crisis is that the trial of strength was symbolic throughout, rather like the manoeuvres of the proverbial Chinese generals of ancient

times. Nobody seriously tried to kill anybody. Perhaps three people
in all actually were killed, though a considerable number were beaten
up.

Whatever happened, both Gaullists and revolutionaries united in
blaming the French Communist Party, either for planning revolution
or for sabotaging it. Neither line of argument is very significant
except as an indication of the crucial role of the CP in May. It was
clearly the only civilian organisation, and certainly the only part
of the political opposition, which kept both its influence and its
head. This is not really surprising, unless we assume that the
workers were revolutionary in the same way as the students, or that
they were as disgusted with the CP.

But though the workers were certainly far more advanced than
their leaders, e.g., in their readiness to raise questions of social
control in industry which the General Labour Federation was
simply not thinking about, the divergences between leaders and
followers in May were potential rather than actual. The political
proposals of the CP almost certainly reflected what most workers
wanted, and quite certainly reflected the traditional mode of
thinking of the French Left (defence of the Republic,' 'union of all
on the left,' 'a popular government,' 'down with one-man rule,' etc):
As for the general strike, the unions had taken it over almost
immediately. Their leaders were negotiating with government and
the bosses, and until they came back with unsatisfactory terms,
there was no reason at all to expect a major revolt against them.
In brief, while the students started their revolt in a spirit of equal
hostility to de Gaulle and the CP (from which most of their leaders
had seceded or been expelled), the workers did not.

The Communist Party was therefore in a position to act. Its
leadership met daily to assess the situation. It thought it knew what
to do. But what was it doing? It was certainly not trying to preserve
Gaullism, for reasons of Soviet foreign policy or any other. As soon
as the overthrow of de Gaulle began to look possible, i.e., between
three and four days after the spontaneous sit-ins started to spread,
it formally staked its own and the popular front's immediate claim
to power. On the other hand it consistently refused to have anything
to do with advocating insurrection, on the grounds that this would
be playing into de Gaulle's hands.

In this it was correct. The May crisis was not a classical
revolutionary situation, though the conditions for such a situation
might have developed very rapidly as a result of this sudden
unexpected break in a régime which turned out to be much more
fragile than anyone had anticipated. The forces of government and
its widespread political support were in no sense divided and
disintegrated, but merely disoriented and temporarily paralysed.
The forces of revolution were weak, except in holding the initiative.
Apart from the students, the organised workers, and some
sympathisers among the college-educated professional strata, their
support consisted not so much in allies as in the readiness of a large
mass of uncommitted or even hostile opinion to give up hope in
Gaullism and accept quietly the only available alternative. As the
crisis advanced, public opinion in Paris became much less favourable
to Gaullism, somewhat more favourable to the old Left, but no clear
preponderance emerges from the public opinion surveys. Had the

Popular Front come, it would certainly have won the subsequent election, just as de Gaulle won his—but victory is a great decider of loyalties.

The best chance of overthrowing Gaullism was therefore to let it beat itself. At one point—between 27 and 29 May—its credibility would have crumbled so much that even its officials and followers might have given it up for lost. The worst policy would have been to give Gaullism the chance of rallying its supporters, the state apparatus, and the uncommitted against a clearly defined, and militarily ineffective, minority of workers and students. Unwilling to expel the striking workers from the factories by force, the army and police were entirely reliable against an insurrection. They said so. And, indeed, de Gaulle recovered precisely because he turned the situation into a defence of 'order' against 'red revolution.' That the CP was not interested in 'red revolution' is another matter. Its general strategy was right for anyone, including revolutionaries, who unexpectedly discovered a chance of overthrowing the régime in a basically non-revolutionary situation. Assuming, of course, that they wanted to take power.

The communists' real faults were different. The test of a revolutionary movement is not its willingness to raise barricades at every opportunity, but its readiness to recognize when the normal conditions of routine politics cease to operate, and to adapt its behaviour accordingly. The French CP failed both these tests, and in consequence failed not only to overthrow capitalism (which it did not want to do just then) but to install the Popular Front (which it certainly did). As Touraine has sarcastically observed, its real failure was not as a revolutionary but even as a reformist party. It consistently trailed behind the masses, failing to recognise the seriousness of the student movement until the barricades were up, the readiness of the workers for an unlimited general strike until the spontaneous sit-ins forced the hands of its union leaders, taken by surprise once again when the workers rejected the terms of strike settlement.

Unlike the non-Communist Left, it was not pushed aside, since it had both organisation and mass support from the grass roots. Like them, it continued to play the game of routine politics and routine labour unionism. It exploited a situation not of its own making, but it neither led nor even understood it, except perhaps as a threat to its own position within the labour movement by the bitterly hostile ultra-Left. Had the CP recognised the existence and scope of the popular movement and acted accordingly, it might just have gained sufficient momentum to force its reluctant allies on the old Left into line. One cannot say much more than this, for the chances of overthrowing Gaullism, though real for a few days, never amounted to more than a reasonable possibility. As it was, it condemned itself, during those crucial days of 27 and 29 May, to waiting and issuing appeals. But at such times waiting is fatal. Those who lose the initiative lose the game.

The chances of overthrowing the régime were diminished not only by the failure of the Communists, but by the character of the mass movement. It had no political aims itself, though it used political phraseology. Without profound social and cultural discontents, ready to emerge at a relatively slight impetus, there can be no major social revolutions. But without a certain concentration on specific targets, however peripheral to their main purpose, the force of such revolutionary energies is dispersed.

It is typical that most of the students themselves (unlike the less revolutionary workers) were not bothered about de Gaulle, except insofar as the real objective, society, was obscured by the purely political phenomenon of Gaullism. The popular movement was therefore either sub-political or anti-political. In the long run this does not diminish its historic importance or influence. In the short run it was fatal. As Touraine says, May 1968 is a less important event in the history of revolutions than the Paris Commune. It proved not that revolutions can succeed in Western countries today, but only that they can break out.

71 · The philosopher:

Jean-Paul Sartre: The New Idea of May 1968

The other day I took part, at the Cité Universitaire, in a debate between students on the possible transformations of the university, and one of them began his speech in this way: 'Comrades, we must recognise that our action during the month of May has been defeated. . . .' A fortnight ago at the Sorbonne, they would not even have let him finish this sentence and he would have been pulled off the platform. This time, there was not one whistle, not one protest: they let him go on.

In a certain sense, in fact, the movement has failed. But it has not failed except for those who believed that the revolution was at hand and that the workers were going to follow the students right to the end, that the action started at Nanterre and in the Sorbonne would end with a social and economic apocalypse which would provoke not only the fall of the régime but the disintegration of the capitalist system. That was a dream and Cohn-Bendit for example never thought that it was the case. He said, on the contrary: 'The revolution will not be made in a day and the union of students and workers will not be brought about tomorrow. We have only taken the first step. We shall be taking others.'

The other day, in fact, at the Cité Universitaire, a Communist came and told us: 'The student movement is not revolutionary because: firstly, it has no revolutionary idealogy; secondly, it has not even shaken the régime; thirdly, it was of an anarchist character because the bourgeoisie in revolt always ends up in anarchy; fourthly, only the workers can make the revolution because they are the producers.'

All that was greeted by boos and whistles, and the poor fellow could scarcely make himself heard, but it was necessary to reply to him. I said this: 'If it's necessary to have a revolutionary ideology in order to make the revolution, then the Cuban Communist Party was the only one that could make it and Castro could not. Now, not only did the Cuban Communist Party not make the revolution but it refused to join in the general strike which was declared at one time by the students and the resistance movement in the towns. What is admirable in the case of Castro is that theory was born from the experience, instead of preceeding it. Re-read the speeches made by Castro before the court which was judging him after the failure of the attack against the barracks at Moncada: you will find in that speech a democratic will to overthrow Batista, because he is a dictator, ideas about social reforms which were still rather vague, but no 'ideological structure'. It was in war itself, in contact with the peasants, that the revolutionary doctrine of Castro was formed. Later, perhaps feeling that his movement was lacking in theoretical basis, he came to terms with the Communists. But when he saw what narrow dogmas they wanted to impose upon him, what mistakes they were making him commit, he reassumed his independence and immediately his ideology was deepened.

The old motor of revolutions, which used to be naked need, has just been succeeded by a new demand, this time for liberty. There was a time when the main problem was that of the collective takeover of the means of production because the ownership and management of industry were in the same hands. That is the period which goes from the birth of family capitalism to the appearance of limited companies and monopolies. It is during this period that the great socialist doctrines were built up. They are all based on the necessity to own property in order to manage it.

Today the middle class has been tranformed by the fact that it can manage without owning. It is the reign of technocracy: the owners, provided that they collect their dividends, delegate to specialists, to competent technicians the trouble of managing the firms. By this very fact the demands we must make have changed their nature: it is no longer the problem of ownership which is in the foreground—that will come up later naturally, because it remains fundamental—but that of power. In the consumer society, people are no longer asking to take over the ownership of things first but to take part in the decisions and to have a measure of control.

My reproach to all those who have insulted the students is that they have not seen that they were expressing the new kind of demand, the demand for sovereignty. In democracy, all men must be sovereign, that is to say they should be able to decide, not alone each in his corner, but all together, what they are going to do. In Western countries this sovereignty only exists on paper: all Americans, including the blacks, are sovereign because they have the right to vote. But they do not have real power and that is why the demand appears for a different power—black power, student power, worker power.

The same thing is true in many of the socialist countries where individuals remain subjected to the necessities of production. It is the students who were the first to feel and formulate all that but they have had sufficient contacts, notwithstanding everything, with the young workers for the latter to be able to say to themselves: 'Why not us? If these fellows can refuse the life which has been arranged for them, why shouldn't we refuse the one which has been arranged for us?' I have a very strong feeling that this refusal of the proletarian condition by young people was the most important novelty of everything that happened in May.

10 · Only a Beginning?

72 · The French political scene in April 1969

On 28 April 1969 de Gaulle lost his referendum on regional devolution and abolition of the Senate: he resigned and in the subsequent election for a new President, the former Gaullist Premier, Georges Pompidou, was the winner. This article sums up the political situation in France a year after the May Events.

**'The Observer,'
27 April 1969**

Why is the General once more in jeopardy less than a year after the student 'revolution' of last May and his subsequent triumphant comeback? The risk of total personal defeat—like the decision to hold the referendum at all—was partly de Gaulle's own choice. He decided that he would resign if he lost the referendum. This helped to dramatise a vote which most Frenchmen otherwise found baffling or boring.

But the fact that the risk has suddenly become real indicates how far the General's position in the country and inside his own party has been shaken since his victory of last summer.

Ironically, the General's present weakness springs as much from the success of the Gaullists in containing and crushing the upheaval last May as from their failure to deal with its underlying long-term causes.

The strength of the conservative reaction to the May revolution, translated into an unprecedented parliamentary majority for the Gaullists at the June elections, underlines in two ways the ultimate appeal de Gaulle has made to public fear. It meant that the choice was no longer simply between his rule and chaos leading to civil war. The shattering blow to the political organisation of the Left and the cautious behaviour of the French Communist Party showed the hollowness of the threat of Communist revolution.

At the same time a serious alternative to the General appeared on the right in the shape of his former Prime Minister and heir presumptive, Georges Pompidou. The firmness and resolution of Pompidou was in marked contrast with the General's fumbling in the early stages of the May crisis. The 'credibility gap' then opened between the General and his traditional supporters was temporarily bridged by de Gaulle's rally and fighting speech, though in the June elections the Gaullist vote was as much for Pompidou as for the General, and more for the concept of law and order than for either.

The gap opened again with de Gaulle's arbitrary dismissal of Pompidou after his election victory. It widened with the economic backlash from the May revolution in the November monetary crisis, the strikes in March and the continued run on the franc.

It began to look as if France's real problems were no longer the dramatic conflicts of divisive colonial revolts. Army mutinies or even left-wing student riots, on which de Gaulle had thrived. They had become, instead, the same kind of humdrum economic and social questions that beset other European countries: essentially how to modernise production and society without inflation, social friction or balance of payments crises. The heroic national gestures of de Gaulle seemed less relevant, and Pompidou had emerged as a ready-make, safe and more up-to-date alternative.

Nor has de Gaulle been able to satisfy the pressure for *participation* and the spirit of *contestation* (questioning) which helped to fire the May revolution, in such a way as to win new support to offset the scepticism of the Right. *Contestation* is one of the enduring legacies of May: nothing in France is taken for granted any more. Even people like the conservative shopkeepers and small industrialists are not frightened to challenge authorities and even to take their problems out into the streets.

Since last May, legislation modernising and liberalising the schools and universities has begun to remove some of the most glaring anomalies in the French education system. But there has been a poor response from the students to participate in the running of the universities, largely because, even under the reformed system, real power still rests with the more conservative teachers and administrators.

Among the students, however, the Government has, by and large, been successful in pulling the moderate reformers away from the left-wing militants. It has been helped by the fragmentation of the breakaway Marxist movements and the dispersal of the student leaders of the May revolution.

For the workers, the biggest gains remain the large pay increases and improved working conditions they secured last June. A profit-sharing measure, compulsory for the larger companies, was recently passed by the Government, but has yet to arouse much enthusiasm on either side of industry.

Since its massive defeat in the Parliamentary Elections last June, and the splintering effect of the May revolution, the Left has still little to show for its efforts to forge a new unity. The referendum has caught it ill-prepared. But a lot of work has been going on, among the Socialists in particular.

A new Socialist Party, drawing in most of the elements which formed the old Federation of the Left, is holding its constituent congress in a fortnight's time. If the new party emerges strong and unified after the congress and can agree with the Communists on a presidential candidate, a Gaullist victory in a new Presidential Election would no longer be a foregone conclusion.

The aim of the younger Socialists is to rid their party of the Old Guard, notably Guy Mollet and his cronies, or at the very least to reduce its power to manageable proportions. It seems probable that a young and dynamic schoolteacher called Pierre Mauroy, who has been very active over the past year in the key political clubs, will be elected president of the party.

The Communist Party unexpectedly is also plucking the fruits of May. Many Marxist heretics disillusioned with their own confusion and disunity have been joining the party on the ground that it does at least represent a tough, organised and determinately anti-Gaullist entity. The party has recorded its highest gains since 1948, 55,000 new members. It has won many new seats on local councils and gained control of several key unions, including the former leftist university teachers' union and a splinter students' union.

73 · The student scene one year later

'The Times,'
18 June 1969

'It's all very simple,' the lecturer in philosophy said. 'We want to destroy the university.' Her pupils applauded warmly. 'It's hard work, but we're making progress. With any luck there won't be any university to come back to in the autumn.'

Mme Judith Miller is intense, serious, a dedicated revolutionary (pro-Chinese), and has an English husband. She teaches at the new experimental university at Vincennes. If the experiment fails it will be largely thanks to her and her friends (Vincennes is the principal power base of the farthest left this year, as Nanterre was last year), and if she fails and Vincennes survives it will be the work of the French Communist Party.

Last year, in the great May cultural revolution, the leftists went to war against the mandarins, the reactionaries, and also against the liberals, moderates and democrats. They won easily, and the whole French university system collapsed.

It has been propped up again, although it is still very shaky indeed, but this year the leftists have much more redoubtable opponents. The presidential elections showed that there are only two really strong political forces in the country, the Gaullists and the communists, and it is only too likely that the leftists are going to be ground to powder between them. They will miss M. Edgar Faure, the Minister of Education, particularly if he is replaced by a really tough Gaullist.

At the moment the communists are making all the running at Vincennes. Elections of student representatives have been held in all the other universities in France, and the communists emerged as the dominant force. The leftists have frustrated elections in Vincennes twice, and if their campaign of disorder prevents the university council from meeting or the university itself from functioning next term it might well be closed. The astonishing new buildings (run up in a few weeks and now housing about 8,000 students) would presumably be handed over to the Army, which can be heard all day shooting merrily away on a range in the woods near by.

Only the most hidebound reactionaries go so far as to say that no degree from any of the Paris universities is worth anything any more, but at any rate the students now have so great a say in the awarding of their degrees and there are so many ways of getting one that all the old certitudes are lost. Potential employers are now inclined to look twice at arts graduates from Paris or its peripheral faculties.

The mandarins wring their hands—but also fight back. The students now enjoy an almost total liberty—they can study what they like, as hard as they like, and conduct as much political activity as they like on the premises. But the lecturers and assistant lecturers have yet to win the same liberty. The autocracy of the 'patrons' was broken last May, but the old guard, which won its way to the top in the old days by clearing a long series of scholastic and administrative hurdles, is clinging to as much of its former authority as it can.

On 19 May a group of deans and professors (including Grappin of Nanterre and Zamansky of the Science Faculty, Paris) issued a stirring declaration to the effect that the national education system and all French universities were on the brink of the abyss. Scenting a counter-revolution, M. Faure issued a counter-declaration which boasted that not a single university institution has been closed this year, listed the reforms and the successes accomplished since 'the events,' and warned that if reaction took control a new revolution would break out.

Some parts of the establishment came through their time of troubles in better shape than others. The English department, for instance, held out longest as a revolutionary centre. None disintegrated more completely than the teaching of art and architecture. The École des Beaux Arts, once the source of all power and patronage (its 'patrons' earned phenomenal sums by monopolizing all the state's architectural work), still subsists because M. Malraux felt charitable towards its teachers. But no one wants to go there any more, and the private schools that prepared students for its entrance examinations are going out of business.

The wave of student militancy has subsided for the moment, and although it could rise up again later the universities and the Ministry of Education are now run with sufficient discrimination to avoid the mistakes made last year when official ineptitude drove the bulk of non-revolutionary students to rally to the militants. There is a degree of sham in the autonomy ostensibly granted to the universities (the Ministry recently decreed who should be rector of Paris and several important provincial universities), but the students no longer feel oppressed.

The only police constantly visible in the Latin Quarter (although there are numerous reserves in the police stations) are not guarding the Sorbonne but the lycées. They haunt the Place de la Sorbonne to keep an eye on St Louis opposite, they patrol Rue St Jacques in large numbers to guard Louis-le-Grand, and they are in constant force around the Pantheon to watch Henri IV.

These huge and forbidding schools, dotted like barracks around the student quarter, are where the real action is this year. The serious fights all take place inside or around the lycées: one boy had his hand blown off by a bomb in Louis-le-Grand. There are constant strikes, riots and fights, and normal discipline had completely broken down.

The student uprising started at Nanterre, the most bourgeois faculty in France. In the lycées, the first schools affected by serious unrest 18 months ago were two of the most snobbish in Paris, Condorcet and Henri IV. At the height of the troubles, a score of Parisian lycées were permanently occupied by their pupils (and these schools may have anything up to 4,000 pupils) and they also formed a large contingent of the barricades.

Discipline in French schools used to be very strict. Now it has collapsed in a great number of Paris lycées (the most recent, severe troubles were at Honoré-de-Balzac) and is barely maintained in numerous others.

The bomb in Louis-le-Grand was thrown by a member of a right-wing commando which broke into the lycée to do battle with the CAL. The rightists were driven out after a fight and the lycée was closed for a few days to let things calm down a little.

For comparison, consider an incident which occurred at Vincennes at about the same time. The leftists noticed an unfamiliar face attending lectures, informed themselves, and discovered it was a notorious rightist called Duprat. He was suspected of belonging to one of the neo-fascist organizations and of accepting police help in compiling a book on the revolutionaries. He was seized, stripped, painted all over with tomato ketchup, and chased naked off the campus. Some girl revolutionaries fainted, thinking it was blood.

Bombs in the lycées, tomato ketchup in the faculties. It looks as though the French educational system has survived another year, but that another explosion is quite on the cards at some future date.

74 · The cost of May

Devaluation of the franc, staved off in November 1968 by de Gaulle's last exercise of political will-power, had finally to be conceded in August 1969, after his resignation.

'The Economist',
16 August 1969

Then came May and June. M. Pompidou lost his premiership by buying out the unions. The Grenelle agreements, raising wage rates as they did by some 15 per cent on an annual basis, presented a difficult problem for the economic managers under the new direction of M. Couve de Murville and M. Ortoli at the finance ministry. But the problem was not impossible. Similar wage explosions had been coped with elsewhere in the common market, notably in Italy and Holland. The considerable slack in the economy, even with the pick-up of production after the dislocation of June, meant that a strategy of rapid expansion had a real chance of success. Higher utilisation of productive capacity would counter the effect of the wage rises on unit costs. Indeed the rise of consumer prices during 1968 was held to 5 per cent. Initially concern over the 1968 budget deficit led to some consumer tax increases. But these were offset by additional subsidies and tax relief for firms, and an expansionist monetary policy. M. Ortoli's budget in October followed the same line, with higher consumer taxes partially offset by a cut in company taxation. At the same time various ad hoc devices were used to keep prices down. On the balance of payments front exports had already received some subsidies, quantitative restrictions were imposed on certain imports and there was a brief period (end-May to early September) of rather ineffective exchange controls.

Then came November, the hurried gathering of finance ministers in Bonn, the haughty refusal of Germany to revalue the D-mark and General de Gaulle's last minute 'no' to devaluation of the franc. The speculative attack on the franc and the general's decision had made the previous policy of expansion an anachronism. Given the irresistible attractions of the undervalued D-mark the franc probably was finished anyway. But undoubtedly poor M. Ortoli made things worse by two bad mistakes. Unlike their British counterparts, the French authorities are not at home with the complexities of exchange control administration. They also suffer from easily bridged frontiers with Switzerland. But really tough controls over monetary movements from June onwards would have checked the outflow of capital, which amounted to $3 billion between June and November. Yet in September the half-hearted exchange controls were removed and simultaneously death duties were doubled: a disastrous package that was bound to swell the capital outflow to a flood. Secondly the government's liberal credit policy, which expanded the money supply formidably encouraged firms to import, and rebuild their stocks. This was a pity. In fact France's trade balance was not as bad as might have been expected. Despite the delays and losses caused by the strikes, exports rose by a healthy 12 per cent over 1968, only slightly out-paced by imports.

Nevertheless, given the refusal of the Germans to revalue, it became a question of when the franc should be devalued, not whether. So French economic policy since November was designed to yield maximum benefit from a devalua-

tion when it should occur, and should be judged accordingly. The post-November package centred round halving the budget deficit, tightening credit severely, and reimposing exchange controls. The strategy was to permit a rather small growth of gnp of around 3.5 per cent in 1969. Unemployment and capacity utilisation would then end the year much where they had been at the end of 1967. Devaluation would then be easy and, given the slack in the economy, advantageous. But this strategy failed. The big fear was that it would be upset by another wage explosion. In the event it was not wages that got out of hand—the unions were ruthlessly and successfully rebuffed at the Rendezvous de Mars. What threatened to push the economy out of control was a consumer boom, fuelled by a run down in personal savings, and backed by a rise in manufacturing investment that now looks like taking it some 25 per cent above last year's level.

At this point the general committed political suicide. After M. Poher's interregnum, when the capital outflow, despite controls, continued to eat into the reserves, M. Pompidou's men did nothing resolutely for a month and then announced some meaningless cuts in public investment plans. But by mid-July the devaluation decision had been taken. The decision was as painful as it was bold for two reasons. One, it overthrew one of the basic tenets of gaullism. Two, it was being taken at a time when the economy was showing every sign of severe overheating. A number of industries were running against capacity, unemployment was still declining, prices were rising at over 6 per cent and the trade gap, although marginally narrower in June, was still large. French industry therefore appeared to be in no shape to benefit from a devaluation. Furthermore, since a fall in the franc is bound to put up prices—by 3 per cent according to official calculations—devaluing in advance of the autumn round of wage negotiations is bound to stiffen the trade unions' demands. Given the state of the French economy, therefore, devaluation has come at the worst possible time. But the government had evidently decided that the situation would not hold until times were better. France has apparently lost $1.8 billion from its reserves since last November. There would be precious little left by December, even

ignoring the impact of a renewed bout of speculation on the D-mark after the German election. And if the franc had to go this year, August—at the height of the holiday season—was obviously the best time.

M. Pompidou's men now have two major challenges. Until the D-mark has been revalued the franc is unlikely to benefit much from favourable capital movements. Internally room has now got to be created for a shift in resources towards exports. France is fortunate here in that the underlying balance is nothing like as bad as it was in Britain during the mid-1960s. An improvement of $400 million to $500 million (see chart) is enough to aim for. This might have been partially achiev-

ed over the next 12 months anyway. French industrial production has now flattened out. The July trade figures show a substantial improvement, and the massive investment boom now looks as if it will taper off next year. The real problem will be to hold wages down. The government has now got to present a new deflationary package in September, and, despite pledges to the contrary, this must involve more taxation. No one can expect a repetition of the 1958–61 experience when real wages did not rise, especially after last year. But they cannot be allowed to increase more than 1-2 per cent (which means 7-8 per cent in money terms). For M. Pompidou's government the real test is still to come.

The Evidence in Pictures

I.   The Peasant Revolt: among the less violent forms of peasant demonstration against the Government in the autumn of 1967 were the attempts to block main roads with surplus farm produce.

II.   Where it all began: the Folly of Nanterre. A drab and functional complex of buildings surrounded by a car park and attended by disgruntled students.

III.   The CRS in action. Their brutality towards the students—and to photographers—made world headlines.

IV.   'Workers and Students, Unite!' The slogan became fact at the Boulogne-Billancourt motor works on the 17th May.

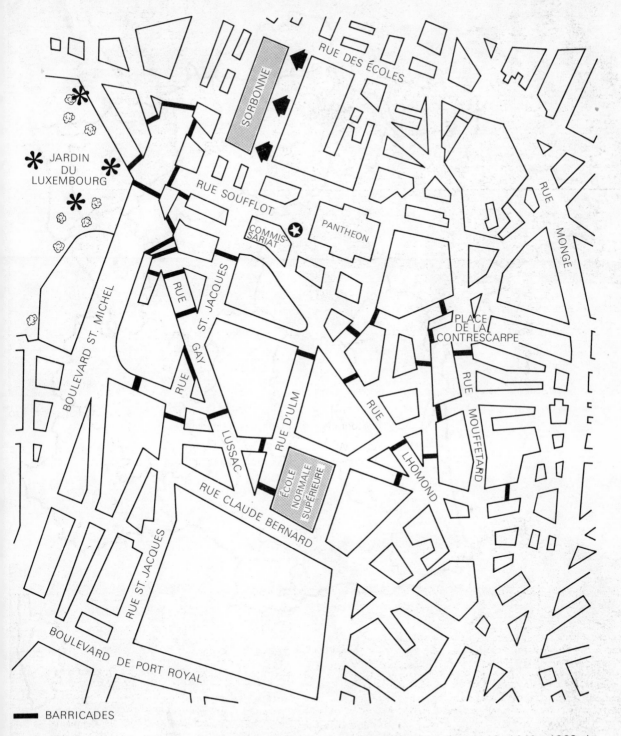

RUE DES ÉCOLES

SORBONNE

JARDIN
DU
LUXEMBOURG

RUE SOUFFLOT

COMMIS-
SARIAT

PANTHEON

RUE MONGE

PLACE
DE LA
CONTRESCARPE

BOULEVARD ST. MICHEL

RUE ST. JACQUES

RUE GAY

RUE D'ULM

RUE

LUSSAC

ÉCOLE
NORMALE
SUPÉRIEURE

LHOMOND

RUE MOUFFETARD

RUE CLAUDE BERNARD

RUE ST. JACQUES

BOULEVARD DE PORT ROYAL

■ BARRICADES

Map of the Quartier Latin showing the barricades on 10–11 May 1968, the
night of the fiercest fighting of all, when over 60 barricades were built, 367
people were taken to hospital, 460 were arrested and 188 cars destroyed.

1 Lille	7 Strasbourg	13 Poitiers	19 Montpellier	25 Cléon	31 Périgueux
2 Amiens	8 Rennes	14 Limoges	20 Marseilles	26 Le Havre	32 St. Brieux
3 Rouen	9 Orléans	15 Clermont-Ferrand	21 Paris	27 Arras	33 Decazeville
4 Caen	10 Nantes	16 Lyon	22 Avranches	28 Vendôme	34 Grenoble
5 Châlons-sur-Marne	11 Dijon	17 Bordeaux	23 Sochaux	29 Le Mans	35 Nice
6 Nancy	12 Besancon	18 Toulouse	24 Flins	30 Quimper	36 Reims

The regions departments and principal towns of France

Appendix

Some Issues

1 Student unrest in France in 1967–8 (pp 3–11)

What justification was there for unrest? Why did it take such an acute form at Nanterre? To what extent did it become political and why? What approach to student grievances was likely to have been more successful in avoiding serious trouble?

2 Students versus police (pp 24–39)

What tactics did the police adopt and why? Could they have been improved? How did the students react to repression? and why? Should they have used different tactics? How did public opinion react? What role did student provocation of the police play in generalising the crisis? Is it possible for governments of the Gaullist type to operate without violence?

3 The strain of economic change (pp 12–17 and pp 41–56)

How was modernisation affecting French industry and agriculture? What were the specific grievances of the workers and peasants? How far were they reflected in the demands made by the Unions? How far was the Great Strike a political phenomenon? How and why was it 'defused' politically? What is the answer to the increasing militancy of industrial workers? What role should Governments play in dealing with it?

4 Gaullism at bay (pp 58–67)

Why did the public lose confidence in the Pompidou government during May? In what ways did the line taken by the PCF affect the action of the Left as a whole, and of the trade unions? How did the anti-Communism of the Right and Centre affect their response to the crisis? How should governments respond to student and industrial unrest? What dangers arise when a government loses touch with public opinion? What are the dangers and advantages of the presidential system of government?

5 The electoral safety-valve (pp 70–76)

Why did the PCF accept the prospect of elections so quickly? Why did de Gaulle's second broadcast succeed when the first had failed? How did the parties try to turn the Events to their advantage in the election campaign? Did the campaign conceal a counter-revolution? Why was the Left beaten so resoundingly only one month after the Events?

6 Long-term implications of the May Events (pp 78–87)

Were the Events a revolution that failed? Was there ever a 'revolutionary situation'? Is revolution possible in the advanced Western countries? What price has France had to pay for the Events? What elements and lessons in the May Events apply to other countries? How important was the existence of a 'revolutionary tradition'? Could it happen here?

Glossary

Abbreviations and French political terms used in this book

CAL: Comité d'action lycéen; schoolboy action committees formed mainly in the lycées.

CDR: Comité de défense de la République; organised by Gaullists for counter-demonstrations etc.

Cinémathèque Française: French National Film Theatre, whose director Henri Langlois had been dismissed earlier by the Gaullist Minister of Culture on political grounds.

Commune, La: the name given to the body set up in Paris in 1871, after defeat of Napoléon III by the Prussians, to try and imitate the Jacobins of 1792. The Commune ruled Paris for seven 'Red Sundays, anticipating certain forms of communism; after starving in the Prussian siege of the city, the Commune was overcome, after a week's savage street battles, by the army of what was to become the Third Republic under Thiers. The bourgeoisie then took its revenge, massacring 20,000 communards on the spot and transporting 7,500 others.

CVN: Comité Vietnam National; a left-wing organisation which led the protest campaign against the war in Vietnam.

CRS: Compagnie républicaine de sécurité; French riot-police descended from a force set up by the collaborationist Vichy government during the war—hence the students' taunt 'CRS—SS'.

CFDT: Confédération française démocratique du travail; the second most powerful trade union group, formerly linked to the Catholic Church.

CGT: Confédération générale du travail; the most powerful trade union group, led by communists.

CIR: Convention des institutions républicaines; the grouping of radical political clubs which acted as a ginger group in the FGDS.

FEN: Fédération de l'enseignment national; right-wing teachers' union.

FER: Fédération des étudiants révolutionnaires; Trotskyite student group, rigidly dogmatic in approach.

FGDS: Fédération de la gauche démocrate et socialiste; Mitterrand's socialist alliance, comprising: Mollet's SFIO, CIR, Radicals.

FNEF: Fédération nationale des étudiants de France; right-wing rival to UNEF.

FO: Force ouvrière; the third most powerful trade union group, split off from CGT when it came under Communist control.

JCR: Jeunesse Communiste révolutionnaire: Trotskyist student group, mostly ex-UEC disillusioned with reformist tendencies of PCF.

lycée: French state secondary school of highly academic type preparing students for the 'baccalauréat', the school-leaving examination which must be passed in order to qualify for university entrance.

MJR: Mouvement de la jeunesse révolutionnaire: fascist student group, offspring of the OAS.

Mouvement du 22 Mars: Cohn-Bendit's Nanterre-based 'spontaneous' alliance of left-wing 'groupuscules' (splinter-groups).

ORTF: Office de radiodiffusion et télévision française: French State broadcasting organisation.

OAS: Organisation de l'armée secrète: terrorist organisation of last-ditch defenders of French Algeria, who made several attempts on de Gaulle's life. Its leaders, jailed or in hiding, were pardoned as part of a deal between de Gaulle and the Army during the May Events.

OCI: Organisation communiste internationaliste: Trotskyist faction not affiliated to the Fourth International (world Trotskyist organisation).

Occident: Right-wing strong-arm youth group.

Patronat, le: Name used to identify French employers' organisations.

PCF: Parti communiste français. French Communist Party.

PCI: Parti communiste internationaliste (French branch of the Trotskyist Fourth International).

PCM-LF: Parti communiste marxiste-léniniste de France; name taken by the Maoists.

PDM: (Centre de) Progrès et démocratie moderne; left-centre group in the National Assembly, led by Jacques Duhamel and Jean Lecanuet, whose tacit support in 1967–8 had enabled the Gaullist government to survive.

PSU: Parti socialiste unifié; small very radical socialist party.

Républicains indépendants: centre-right supporters of Valéry Giscard d'Estaing, collaborated with the Gaullists in the Assembly.

SFIO: Section française de l'internationale ouvrière; Guy Mollet's moderate socialists.

Situationnistes: student group of nihilistic surrealists—responsible for many slogans, posters and graffiti during the Events.

SNESup.: Syndicat national de l'enseignement supérieur; Left-wing led university teachers union.

UDR: Union pour la défense de la République (subsequently Union des démocrates pour la République) name used by the Gaullists during 1968 election campaign.

UD Vème: Union des démocrates pour la cinquième République; name used by the Gaullists prior to the May Events.

UEC: Union des étudiants communistes; official Communist students movement.

UJCM-L: Union de la jeunesse communiste marxiste-léniniste; Maoist rival to UEC.

UNEF: Union nationale des étudiants de France; main French student union, left-wing controlled.

Key to political leanings of French newspapers and weeklies

L'Aurore	Right-wing independent, critical of Gaullists.
Combat	Left-wing independent
Le Figaro	Centre-right independent; an establishment paper, usually supporting the Gaullists.
L'Humanité	Organ of the PCF.
La Nation	Organ of the Gaullists.
Le Monde	An institution rather than a newspaper, giving total coverage of all political news and balanced commentary: critical of Gaullism but not prejudiced against it.
Le Parisien Libéré	Right-wing independent.
L'Express	Centre-left independent imitation of **Time**.
Le Nouvel Observateur	Intellectual left-wing.

Sources of documents

1 Nesta Roberts: *Guardian*, 22 February 1968
2 Yvon Le Vaillant: *Le Nouvel Observateur*, 2 February 1968
3 *L'Évènement*, February 1968
4 Student leaflet
5 Maurice Merleau-Ponty, Professor of Epistemology, Nanterre: *Le Nouvel Observateur*, 13 March 1968
6 Student leaflet
7 Norman Macrae: *The Economist*, 18 May 1968
8 Gretton: *Students and Workers*, (Macdonald 1969)
9 Seale and McConville: *French Revolution 1968*, (Penguin 1968)
10 *L'Express*, 15 April 1968
11 Lucien Rioux: *Le Nouvel Observateur*, 13 February 1968
12 Georges Suffert and others: *L'Express*, 9 October 1968
13 a) Gretton: op.cit.
   b) Seale and McConville: op. cit.
   c) Seale and McConville: op. cit.
14 Patrick Brogan: *The Times*, 30 May 1968
15 Pierre Viansson-Ponté: *Le Monde*, 15 March 1968
16 B. Girod de L'Ain: *Le Monde* 8 May 1968
17 Peter Lennon: *Guardian, 29 May 1968*
18 Paul Johnson: *New Statesman*, 24 May 1968
19 Katia Kaupp: *Le Nouvel Observateur*, 19 June 1968
20 Rene Backmann: *Le Nouvel Observateur*, 19 June 1968
21 Paul Johnson: *New Statesman*, 17 May 1968
22 Quoted in Gretton, op. cit.
23 Student leaflet
24 Eye witness and press sources
25 *Le Nouvel Observateur*, 15 May 1968
26 Alain Touraine, Professor of Sociology, Nanterre: *Le Monde*, 11 May 1968
27 a) *Le Monde*, 8 May 1968
   b) *Le Monde*, 11 May 1968
   c) *Le Monde*, 12 May 1968
28 a) *Le Monde*, 7 May 1968
   b) *L'Humanité*, 8 May 1968
   c) *L'Humanité*, 12 May 1968
29 *Le Monde*, 10/11 May 1968 }
30
31 *Le Monde*, 12 May 1968 }
32
33 *L'Humanité*, 11 May 1968
34 a) *Le Figaro*, 5 May 1968
   b) *Le Combat*, 7 May 1968
   c) *Le Parisien Libéré* 7 May 1968
   d) *L'Aurore*, 7 May 1968
   e) *L'Express*, 13 May 1968
35 *The Economist*, 25 May 1968
36 *The Times*, 20 May 1968

37 a) Quoted in Gretton, op.cit.
   b) *The Economist*, 1 June 1968
   c) K. S. Karol: *New Statesman*, 31 June 1968
38 Seale and McConville: op.cit.
39 Hella Pick: *Guardian*, 30 May 1968
40 *The New York Times*, 17 May 1968
41 J. P. Talbo: *La Grève à Flins* (Maspero 1968)
42 Quoted in Gretton; op.cit.
43 *Le Combat*, 24 May 1968
44 *Le Monde*, 23 and 24 May 1968
45 *L'Humanité*, 17, 21 and 26 May 1968
46 *The Times*, 25 May 1968
47 *Le Monde*, 26 May 1968
   L'Humanité, 26 May 1968
48 *Daily Telegraph*, 25 May 1968
49 a) *Pravda*, 28 May 1968
   b) New China News Agency, 27 May 1968
   c) *The New York Times*, 25 May 1968
   d) *The Times*, 25 May 1968
50 Mervyn Jones, *The New Statesman*, 27 June 1968
51 *Le Monde*, 29 May 1968
52 *Le Monde*, 29 May 1968
53 *Daily Telegraph*, 31 May 1968
54 *Le Monde*, 28 May 1968
55 Found in Paris street, 30 May 1968
56 *L'Humanité*, 27 May 1968
57 *Le Monde*, 29 May 1968
58 *Le Monde*, 30 May 1968
59 *L'Humanité*, 29 May 1968
60 *Le Monde*, 30 May 1968
61 *The Times*, 31 May 1968
62 *L'Humanité*, 31 May 1968
63 *Le Figaro, Le Combat, La Nation*, 31 May 1968; *Le Monde*, 1 June 1968
64 Seale and McConville, op.cit.
65 Charles Hargrove: *The Times*, 8 and 12 June 1968
66 *Le Monde*, 6 June 1968
67 *L'Humanité*, 8 June 1968
68 Gretton, op.cit.
69 a) *L'Humanité*, 24 June 1968
   b) *Le Combat*, 24 June 1968
   c) *Le Monde*, 2 July 1968
   d) *Le Nouvel Observateur*, 3 July 1968
   e) *The New York Times*, 1 July 1968
   f) *The Times*, 2 July 1968
70 *New York Review*, 22 May 1969
71 Jean-Paul Sartre, *Le Nouvel Observateur*, 26 June 1968
72 Robert Stephens and John St Jorre: *The Observer*, 27 April 1969
73 Patrick Brogan: *The Times*, 18 June 1969
74 *The Economist*, 16 August 1969